Nothin

Recent Poetry in Cornish

Edited by Tim Saunders

Nothing Broken

Recent Poetry in Cornish

Preface by Alan Llwyd

Francis
Boutle
Publishers

First published by Francis Boutle Publishers
272 Alexandra Park Road
London N22 7BG
Tel/Fax +44 (0)20 8889 7744
Email: info@francisboutle.co.uk
www.francisboutle.co.uk

ISBN 1 903427 30 4

Printed by Biddles Ltd.

Acknowledgements

I would like to thank all the poets who kindly submitted their work to this collection. I would also like to thank the editors of books and journals, especially *Delyow Derow*, and earlier collections in which several of these poems first appeared. To Ceri and Meirion – my thanks for their patience while this anthology was in development. My thanks also to Tony Hak for his help. Finally, I would like to thank Dr Alan M. Kent for his invaluable input and advice on this volume.

To John Bolitho 1930–2005

Contents

Preface

Even when I visited Cornwall almost a decade ago, on a family holiday, I never once thought of Cornwall as being part of England, or Pow Sows. We stayed at Porthia (St Ives), and a visit to Pedn an Wlas (Land's End) was a must. Tourists are tourists everywhere! We had already spent many holidays in the South of England, and we knew that we were in England. Cornwall was different from the moment we arrived. Houses, hotels and streets had names which I could immediately recognise. Travelling by bus to Land's End I noticed the name of a farm near the sea on a weather-beaten gate. It was 'Mor Garow' I didn't even have to translate the words in my mind. I knew exactly what they meant, and I was almost reading my own language 'môr garw' ('rough sea'). That holiday was a rich, but frustrating, experience.

I had already been impressed by Cornish poetry long before I was asked to write a preface to *Nothing Broken*. I have read *The Wheel: An anthology of modern poetry in Cornish 1850-1980*, also edited by Tim Saunders, and Saunders' own collected poems in Cornish, *The High Tide*, several times. This anthology maintains the standard of its predecessors, and also introduces new voices. New voices are always an indication that a language is growing. One thing that has struck me about the three collections is that the poems are real poems by real poets, not poetic exercises in a minority language, or an attempt to give a small, revived language a body of contemporary work. The poets do not write to give credence to the language; it is the language itself that gives credence to their work. The emphasis is still on the word 'modern', not merely 'modern' as in 'contemporary' but also modern in style, concept and outlook. A great many of the poems included in these anthologies could have easily fitted into a modern European anthology such as Daniel Weissbort's *The Poetry of Survival*, an anthology of poems by post-war poets of central and eastern Europe. One thing that has struck me about recent Cornish poetry is that no effort has been made to rebuild a lost tradition. It has been a sudden leap into modern poetry, often using contemporary themes, subjects and topics, which shows that the language has confidence and optimism. Here we have poems about Bush and Blair, Kosovo, mobile phones and urban vandalism. Cornish is a modern language. As Graham Sandercock says in his poem 'Poll Pri' ('Clay Pit'):

> So easy, very easy,
> it is to look backwards
> to past ages,
> at the history of the country;
> would it be of any use
> to retread the footsteps,
> footprints born,
> in the country's history?

Threatened languages look to the past for inspiration. Rather than retrace their footsteps in the country's past, Cornish poets have taken their 'first tentative steps in Kernow', as Cliff Stephens says in 'An Divres' ('The Exile'):

> Yet, the flame remains alive,
> Lying dormant deep within the soul
> Until it re-ignites
> Rising like a phoenix
> From the ashes of despair
> To shine like a beacon
> Guiding the way
> On a journey of rediscovery.
> A pilgrimage to the old country
> And the first tentative steps in Kernow
> Bring a sudden rush of emotion,
> A joyous reunion,
> Like a lost child, found
> Held in its mother's loving arms,
> A sense of belonging,
> At last,
> I've come home.

This anthology is, indeed, 'a joyous reunion', and these first tentative steps have become confident strides. A revived language such as Cornish can only look to the future. Nothing has really been broken, or at least nothing that couldn't be repaired. Cornish has been repaired. Judging from this anthology, nothing was really lost in the first place.

Many of the poems in this book are, inevitably, concerned with identity and with the Cornish language itself, such as 'Geryow Kernewek' ('Cornish Words') by Donald R. Rawe, who has other excellent poems in the book; another is 'An Taves Hen' ('The Old Language') by Julyan Holmes, which seems to me to be quite an accomplished poem, especially from the metrical point of view; and there are others, such as 'Pysadow rag an Naw Kans' ('Prayer for the Nine Hundred') by Judith Larham, another fine poem, hard-hitting as it is, and 'Na Wra Omblegya' ('No Surrender') by Cliff Stephens, 'Yeth Ow Thas' ('My Father's Language') by Gari Retallack, and 'Leav an Nyer Le' ('Minority Report') and the satirical 'Kernopalooza Rap' by Alan M. Kent. To single out poems which have impressed me would give a wrong impression; every single poem has impressed me in one way or another. But I will mention two names. I read poems by Tony Snell in *The Wheel*, and they created a lasting impression on me. He is well-represented here, as he should be, and has again given us some wonderful poems, especially 'Night Run' and 'Nothing Broken', which has given the anthology its title. And there is Saunders himself, whose poems always excite me. 'An Pennlanw' ('The High Tide') is quite an accomplishment, and it is interesting to note, from a Welshman's viewpoint at least, that his 'An Ros Du' is based on the Welsh Englynion Beddau ('Englynion of the Grave'). These two would stand out in any modern European language.

Reading these collections has certainly enriched my life. I find myself reading the poems in both languages, slowly. Being able to discover the meaning of whole lines, and even a whole verse in one instance, without conferring with their English counterparts, excites me. I feel that am I getting to know another language. And yet it's a frustrating experience. I feel that I should learn the language, and that I could learn the language in a comparatively short time. But we in Wales, like our Cornish cousins, have to work hard to preserve, protect and enhance our own language, and time is more than precious. And yet, the Welsh should really make an effort to learn their sister-language and add to continually growing number of Cornish speakers. This is a major anthology in a minority language, and not only because of the poetry.

Alan Llwyd

Introduction

Nothing Broken takes up the story of Cornish poetry where my anthology *The Wheel* left off – in 1980, just as the Cornish language and literature were about to undergo a rapid change. About that time a group of activists around the magazine *An Gannas* introduced a new generation to the language and effectively created a new public for Cornish poetry as well as new writers who think and feel in Cornish. The language articulates their personal experience, gives voice to national aspirations and expresses their concerns over universal themes. They hear Cornish poetry shouted over the din of pubs and exchange poems by email. Favourite pieces are often sung by their authors. Children's rhymes and songs are multiplying and two new journals *Bardhonieth Kernow/Poetry Cornwall* and *Scryfa* take writing in Cornish to the next generation of readers.

Echoes of traditional poetry now come unforced – sometimes quite unconsciously. Free verse remains popular, but some poets also experiment with classical Celtic prosody. The prospect of official status for Cornish and of a place in the school curriculum offers exciting possibilities. The average age of the audience for Cornish poetry will drop, as will the average age of the poets themselves. The future of the language seems, if not assured, full of a hope unimaginable a generation ago.

This anthology does not set out to be comprehensive. The older kind of romanticism displays too little originality to earn much space here. Children's verse now merits an anthology of its own and Cornish song is so widespread that the most highly selective collection would take up several CDs.

It is my intention to let the poems speak for themselves and so I have not included more than a couple of notes. Biographies of the authors are at the back, along with the sources of the poems. There is a comprehensive bilbiography for readers interested in the linguistic, cultural and historical background to modern Cornish poetry.

Once again it is a pleasure to name an anthology after a poem by Tony Snell, who has not only handed on a tradition to us: he has refined and extended it. We await with impatience the appearance of his own collected poems.

With the publication of *Looking at the Mermaid*, *The Wheel* and now *Nothing Broken*, the reader can form a view of Cornish poetry from the earliest records up to the present day. The work has been hard, but it has been a real joy. Now, perhaps, it is time for something else ...

Tim Saunders
Gabalfa, 2006

The Poems

Wella Brown

Nerth Medhel

Gans freuth ha fros an tonnow down ha glas
a herdh yn rew erbynn an alsoyow bras.
Skantlowr y hyll an keynvor fedha men,
kyn treyla oesow pell a-dro, mes den,
a with y golon saw gans fosow serth,
a woer y fydhons skwerdys prest dre nerth
unn wolok vludh ha glew ow lamma skon
dhiworth dewlagas hag a'n feth dison.

Soft Strength

With violent and tumultuous currents, the deep green waves
thrust one after another at the great cliffs.
The ocean can scarcely defeat stone
although long ages pass, but man
who guards his heart securely with steep walls
knows that these will be rent by the strength
of one soft and clear look, leaping quickly
from a pair of eyes and conquering him immediately.

Richard Gendall

An Yrth

Pe ra ve settya an trooz en garrack looez,
pokeean an vethan welgack, po en vor,
po war an treath ew golhez gan an moar,
me ore tel era ve a savall,
kenz leb reeg savall leeas orol,
ha vedn gweel andelha arta.
An stennar, eve aweath,
palas dreath an doar,
kethew an kenza,
na ell e boaz seere tha voaz dewetha
leba tene eve e whath.

Buz an yrth,
cothes thur an ebbarn,
gwidn, glane, elyn, ytava an dro,
ha pe re ve merkya e landar cro
tranformya an mena dyckles
leba therea ve a kerras,
serten ew dro ve an kensa,
tra vethama aweath dewetha,
rag scoen pub vollan ra boaz kellez,
thethez tha veaz, devethez dowre,
ha gonga keniffer ooll ve gwrez
genam war e vedgath flowre.

The Snow

When I set foot upon the grey rock,
or else on the grassy meadow, or on the road,
or on the beach that is washed by the sea,
I know that I stand
where before have stood many others,
and will do so again.
The tinner, he too,
digging through the ground,
though he is the first
cannot be sure to be the last
where he draws his breath.

But the snow,
fallen from the sky,
white, clean, bright, there it is all around,
and when I note its fresh cleanness,
transforming the bleak hillside
where I walk,
it is certain that I am the first,
that I shall also be the last,
for soon each flake will be lost,
melted away, turned to water,
and with it every trace that has been made
by me upon its matchless face.

Moaz Lowz

Tho ve scathe
nevra war an moer a neidga,
gen an todnow leskez,
gen an gwendgow heltheze...
na oar den'eth gwelhas
plea reeg ve kerras.

Tho ve quillan
war askall goolan,
pup ear pell a vaggia
pelea vo da gonga,
ubma ha enna,
skesy nevra
ha nan veth.

Cran o ve,
nevra andro therama a moaz,
nag eze dallath,
nag eze duath,
della me re boaz
tereba merwall:
Dew gwerras thebm a fall.

Adrift

I am a boat
ever on the sea drifting,
by the waves rocked,
by the winds driven...
no man can see
where I have gone.

I am a feather
on a gull's wing,
ever travelling far
where it pleases her,
here and there,
never shall I be able
to escape.

I am a circle,
ever around I go,
there is no beginning,
there is no ending,
thus shall I be
until I die.
God help me in my failure.

Stearen Lesky

Me zavas dadn an ebbarn clere an noze,
Settez oll andro gen sterrez gulow,
Anella whath an delkiow
Cregy bith mar guzal an gweeth ethez.

Therr edn stearen mesk angye
Passia, ha gonz aise, tectar an rerol,
O gwidn, o glaze, o gwear, oyracke, entye,
"Meer, ottave!" hevely laull.

Na olgama tha veaz trailia a goolack,
Glenez prest urt hye sevilliack,
Buz wharea me as gwelhas hye
Killynia tua ve precarra lagas lesky.

He me reeg poonia raage,
A doola stous deraage,
Ha e hatsha nenna,
Ha e sendgy en ma devra,
Buz, ah! hye loskas, hye loskas,
Hye loskas tidn heb truath ry,
Ha lesky meaz an golan ve.

Shooting Star

I stood beneath the clear sky of the night,
Set all about with bright stars,
Breathing in the breath of the leaves
Hanging ever so still on the scented trees.

There was one star among them
That surpassed with ease the beauty of the others,
Which was white, blue, green, golden for sure,
"Look, here I am!" it seemed to say.

I could not turn away my gaze,
Ever clinging to her unmoving,
But presently I saw her
Slanting towards me like a burning eye.

And I ran forward,
My hands outstretched,
And caught her then,
And clasped her to my breast,
But oh! she burnt, she burnt,
She burnt painfully, mercilessly,
And burnt away my heart.

Ula an Cooz

Ha me a moaz en kerras
Tua an drea,
Edn metten have arvis,
Tha dowla lether mouy en poss,
Abew an kea,
Enna drez am scooth, me glowas
Hubbadullia mesk an ethen...
Mola looz ha due, ha gwradnan,
Ruddock, tink, pednplay, gulvan...
Pandra whear? ter me an breze.
Eze neb edn pye, po brane, po cathe,
Gwiwer, po nepeth orrol,
Ladra oyow meaz an neith?

Thosympyas me an gwelhas,
En bar zeah clugia... Ula!
Cuzal, tewl, misticall.
You! metha ve, scantlowar metha
Tha anella,
Ass o che teag!
Ha trailia an dro e bedn,
Ha merkia ve
Dreath an drokow e legadgow,
Carra wherthin, ameth e:
"Peea che behatna, boya,
Tho che an kednow ve an journama!"

The Wood Owl

As I was walking
Towards the village,
One morning early in summer,
To put another letter in the post,
Above the hedge,
There over my shoulder, I heard
An uproar among the birds...
Thrush and blackbird, and wren,
Robin, finch, titmouse, sparrow...
What's up? I think to myself,
Is there some magpie, or crow, or cat,
Squirrel, or something else,
Stealing eggs from a nest?

Suddenly I saw him,
On a dry branch perching... An Owl!
Still, inscrutable, mysterious.
Hi there! says I, hardly daring
To breathe.
Aren't you beautiful!
And turning his head around,
And marking me
Through the slits of his eyes,
As if laughing, he says:
"If you had been smaller, my lad,
You'd have been my dinner this day!"

Richard Jenkin

Yma Cowas Ow-tegensewa

"Yma ow-tegensewa
Hager gowas, war ow feth." – Origo Mundi

Yndella kens Cam a leverys
    Hag ef ow-queles dos lyf dowr
May fudhys ynno oll an norvys.
    Ena glaw whar dhe sethow dur
O trelyes, an bewnans oll yn bys
    Dhe ladha, gwyskys scon dhe'n lur –
Den, benen, mylas ha losowys –
    Oll marow ma's remenant lowr
A-ve rynnys yn gorhel gans Noy
    Rak dalleth arta denythy,
Herwyth aga hynda, bewnans moy.
    Dre dhowr Ancow a-wruk myjy
Trevas vrassa y'n bys. Dhyn dew roy
    Ny dhe weles nep marthusy
Mar uthek 'vello nefra na moy
    Rak own a vernans oll dhyn-ny.
Mes pyu a wor an pyth a whyrfyth?
    Us ow-tegensewa lemmyn
Hager gowas warnan hag a vyth
    Moy uthek 'esso yn termyn
A-dhe, ow-casa yn-few travyth?
    Cowas tan a nef y-whelyn,
– Mylweth es lughesen, war ow fyth, –
    Mernans hager gans paynys tyn.
Y-fythyn golyes gans golow,
    Y lugh ow-lesky pup lagas.
Yn pols munys gans tomder Howlow
    Enawys 'vyth agan dyllas.
Enawel a-wheth dhe-ves trevow,
    Ow-ton breghy gans bros cudhys

A Shower is Looming

"There is looming
An ugly shower, by my faith." – Origo Mundi

It was thus that Ham spoke
    As he saw a flood of water coming
In which all the world was drowned.
    Then gentle rain into steel needles
Was turned, all the life in the world
    To be killed, swiftly struck to the ground
– Man, woman, animals, plants –
    All dead apart from a sufficient remainder
Borne in a ship by Noah
    To start regenerating again,
According to their kind, more life.
    Through water Death reaped
The greatest harvest in the world. May God grant us
    That we never see any wonder
So terrible ever again
    For fear of death to us.
But who knows what will happen?
    Is there now looming
An ugly shower which will be
    More terrible than this in time
To come, leaving nothing alive?
    A shower of fire from heaven we shall see,
– A thousand times more than lightning, truly, –
    An ugly death with bitter pains.
We shall be wounded by light,
    Its flash burning every eye.
In a tiny moment the heat of Suns
    Will ignite our clothes.
A storm will blow towns away,
    Bringing débris covered in burning

A goth yn glaw ha gwana gwlasow,
 Tan atom pan dheffo dhe'n bys.

That will fall in rain and lacerate countries,
    When the fire of the atom comes to the world.

Lef y'n Nos

Ha my ow-crowedha y'm gwely,
Y clewys-vy lef whek y'n nos,
Ow-whystra yn cosel hag ysel
"Ow herra, a vynta-jy dos
Dres anken hag ober hep deweth
Dhe bowes yn cres a buptra
A drobel dha vewnans gans drokter?
Y hyllyth-sy cuska yn-ta
Hep covyon a dhregyn adro dhys.
Rak hunlef ha preder mar dhown
Y'th whythaf." "Pyu osta?" a gryys.
"A goweth, yth of-vy Annown."

26

Voice in the Night

As I was lying in my bed,
I heard a sweet voice in the night,
whispering softly and low:
"My dearest, do you want to come
Beyond grief and endless work
To rest in peace from everything
That troubles your life with evil?
You can sleep well
Without memories of mischief around you.
From nightmare and so deep care
I will guard you." "Who are you?" I cried.
"O friend, I am Annown."

Annown: the abode of the dead.

Jowann Richards

Kan an Vowes Yowynk

Ow harer eth dhe ves,
    Yn termyn Kynyav hweg;
Eve eth ha bos soudor,
    Den yowynk, krev ha teg.

Dres Gwav ny'n gwelis vy,
    Yn kewer yeyn ha garow;
Y tybis vy ow harer
    Dhe vos martesen marow.

Yeyn ena o ow horf,
    Ha yeyn ynwedh ow brys:
Y fia men ow holonn
    Mar ny ve hwath y'n bys.

Y teuth wor'tiwedh Gwenton,
    Ny res dhymmo vy keudhi:
Re dheuth dhymmo ow harer,
    Ay! Ass wrug ev ow theudhi!

Song of the Young Girl

My lover went away,
    In the sweet autumn time;
He went to be a soldier,
    A young man, strong and fine.

Throughout the winter I did not see him,
    In weather cold and rough;
I thought that my lover
    Perhaps was dead.

Cold then was my body,
    And cold also my mind:
My heart would be stone
    If he were not in the world.

At last there came the spring,
    No need for me to grieve,
My lover has come back to me;
    O! How he thawed me!

Ann Trevenen Jenkin

Hal Dart

An hal yu compes
Gell, ha gwer ha du;
An dor gwernak yu
Adro an veyn growyn.

Blejennow byghan yu gwelys
Sterennow melen splan
Adro meyn elevennek
Yn gwelsennow gun.

Tykkydew gans lyes lyw
A-nyj yn ebren splan;
An comolow gwyn a-nuf
Avel an deves bugales.

Gwyngala, an dalleth Kynyaf
An delyow a-wra cotha
An deweth Haf tom –
Pan dhe'n Gwaf.

Dartmoor

The moor is level,
Brown and green and black
The ground is marshy
Around the granite stones.

Little flowers are seen
Fine yellow stars
Around the stones of elvan
On the grassy moor.

A butterfly of many colours
Flies in the splendid sky
The white clouds float
Like the sheep of the shepherd.

September, the start of autumn,
The leaves fall,
The end of a hot summer –
And then comes winter.

Mernans

Nyns yu possybl dhe serry yn-fras adro mernans
Nyns yu travyth a leverel
Marder, muvyansow, cref, kerensa
A-wra agan don dres oll an jeth.

Mes an sor y whraf-vy synsy bos rak
Taclow goky – nagonen dh'ygery sten
Dhe wolghy an cheny gwell agesof.
Gortheby an darras dyworth a-bell.

Nyns us genef-vy denvyth genef bos serry
Po serry yn-fras erbyn bys camkensek
Nyns yu nagonen dh'omgusulya
Adro geryow crowsek po yeth Kernow
Po dhe weles baner Pyran yn-stowt dysplegys.

Nyns yu nagonen parusy rag prysyow specyal
Po cara rak an taclow sempel,
Dybry y yos kergh yn furf Crows Keltek
Ombredery war hembrynkysy Geltek
Po myghterneth Kernow.

Nyns yu nagonen dhe gewsel orth ha my ow-tos tre
Po govyrn adro scodhyans cuf
Nyns yu nagonen dhe ranna lowender po galarow
Ha prevyansow hudhyk po domhelans.

Ny vyth nefra bos nagonen ow-tos
Nagonen rak ygery an darras
Nefra ha nagonen rak gwytha
Nefra, soweth, nefra namoy.

Death

One cannot rage over death –
There is nothing to say
Numbness, strong emotions, love
Carry us through the day.

But the anger I feel is for
Stupid things – no-one to unscrew a jar,
To wash up better than I,
To answer the door from afar.

I have no-one with me to be angry
Or to rage at
an unjust world
No-one to consult over cross-words or Cornish
Or to see St Piran's flag proudly unfurled.

No-one to prepare special meals for
Or to love for the simple things
Eating his porridge in the shape of a Celtic cross,
Musing on Celtic leaders
or great Cornish kings.

No-one to talk to on returning
Or to ask for friendly support
No-one to share joy or mourning
And experiences happy or fraught.

There will never be anyone coming
No-one to open the door
Never and no-one for caring
Never alas, never no more.

Donald R. Rawe

An Skyla dhe Vos

Pan welaf an gonys a'n scryforyon,
Pregowthoryon dre osow hyr,
Ha fatel y re-dheweth aga fewnans oll
Hag ynweth py dader y a wruk
Rak oll-ny omma, a yllyf ola,
Ola rak an dhrok yu genen whath,
Ola rak agan fleghes ha dyeskynysy:
Omma yu mernans, clafter, hakter,
Tus yn pryson tewlys gans cam,
Moreth ha ponvotter war tu.

Erigena, den fur, a gews whath,
Ynweth Pascal, Montesquieu, Shaw,
Socrates, Ghandi ha Syrra Thomas More.
Mes ny a-s-ankev oll hemma
Yn agan sewyanslust ha hebasca,
Ow whylas agan les agan honen:
An bys yu fol, y-grysaf menough.

Mes pan brederaf ahanas, ow hares ger,
Pan berthaf cof dha dheulagas len,
Dha dhyvron whek ha dha dhywvregh cref,
Oll dygolon 'wra tremena.
Kerensa yu agan gwayntyans unyk,
Agan daspren lel, agan skyla dhe vos:
Ny a vew rag cara, nyns yu gwyr?
Glenyn an yl y gyla, yndella:
Nefra ny dyberthyn na vewyn a-les,
Erna ny eth dhe'n tewlder warbarth,
Dhe'n deweth agan bys ha termyn...

The Reason for Being

When I see the work of writers,
Preachers through the ages long
And how they all ended their lives
And also what good they did
For us all here, I could weep,
Weep for the evil that is with us still,
Weep for our children and descendants:
Here are death, sickness, hatred,
People thrown into prison wrongfully,
Sorrow and trouble on all sides.

Erigena, wise man, speaks still.
Also Pascal, Montesquieu, Shaw,
Socrates, Ghandi and Sir Thomas More.
But we forget all these
In our pursuit of lust and comfort,
Seeking our own profit.
The world is mad, I often think.

But when I think of you, my dear friend,
When I remember your trusting eyes,
Your sweet breast and strong arms,
All faintheartedness passes.
Love is our only hope,
Our true redemption, our reason for living:
We live to love, is it not true?
Let us cleave to one another, therefore;
Never let us separate or live apart;
Until we go into the darkness together,
To the end of our world and time...

Pysadow rak Kernow yn Vledhen 2000 [esrann]

AGAN TAS NY US YN NEF, BENYGYS REBO DHA HANOW:
RE DHEFFO DHA WLASCOR
Nyns us nef war nor, Arluth,
Ny a vynnes gul, ty a wor,
Mes bewnans gwell rak agan pobel,
Bewnans heb drok ha fowt skyans,
Bewnans dhe wothvos agan tyr-ma
Yn y splander ha'y velder,
Hep cost gwryans crefny,
Bewnans rak agan fleghes dhe dryga
Hep own ny nown anken,
Nanyl dyvroeth constrynys, kepar ha lemmyn.
A Arluth ker, clew agan pysadow.

DHA VOTH REBO GWRES Y'N NOR KEPAR HAG YN NEF
Omma yn nor, war an gweras, may fyth kerensa
Yn mysk oll, ha both da ynweth;
Cres war oll agan bys-ma, war trevow
Ha cyta, hal ha meneth.
Ny a vyn tryga yn-dan dha woskes, Arluth,
Nag ow stryva rak les agan honen,
Mes ow cul dader yn dha wel.

RO DHYN-NY HEDHYU AGAN BARA PUP TETH OLL
Ow thas-vy, eth bledhen y os, reseth dhe'n scol
Yn eskyjow y whor, y hansel hernen wyn holanek –
Deudhek rak an dynar ena. An morlenwel a vudhys
Kegyn ow Mamwyn. Ow Thaswyn revys kebellans scath
Dyworth Lanwednock dhe Garrek Du, bledhen war bledhen,
Banna rhum rak hansel; ha merwys, pur goth kens y dermyn,
Hanter cans ha deu bloth.
Agan mowysy a dre a gerthys an forthow y'n nor,
A blegys an Squyr ha'y vebyon
Rak sols py deu; ha Marya MacDelen eth gans marners
War'n cayys Lanwednok. Ow kerdhes dhe Dolcoath
Jowan Harris re scryf vardhonnygow
Yn sugan mor du:
'Nefra ny-welas-sy bal? Dus genef-vy.'

Prayer for Cornwall in the Year 2000 [extract]

*OUR FATHER, WHICH ART IN HEAVEN, HALLOWED BE
THY NAME; THY KINGDOM COME*
It is not heaven on earth, Lord,
We would make, Thou knowest,
But a better life for our people:
A life without ignorance,
A life to know this our land
In its splendour and sweetness,
Free of selfish grasping:
A life for our children to live
Without fear or hunger
Nor enforced exile, as it is now.
O dear Lord, hear our prayer.

THY WILL BE DONE ON EARTH, AS IT IS IN HEAVEN
Here on this soil, that there may be love
Amid all and goodwill also:
Peace over all our world, over villages
And city, moor and mountain.
We wish to live under your protection, Lord,
Not striving for our own gain
But doing good in thy sight.

GIVE US THIS DAY OUR DAILY BREAD
My father, eight years old, went to school
In his sister's shoes; a salt herring for breakfast –
Twelve a penny then. The high tide flooded
My grandmother's kitchen. My granddad rowed the ferry
From Padstow to Rock, year after year,
A tot of rum for breakfast, and died, old before his time,
Fifty two years of age.
Our town girls walked the streets at night,
Pleased the Squire and his sons, for a shilling or two;
And Mary MacDellan went with sailors
On the docks of Padstow. Walking to Dolcoath,
John Harris wrote his poems down
In blackberry juice:
'Hast ever seen a mine? Come with me.'

'Yn dan o cavyow garow gans tewlder craf.'
Lucretia a verwys, wek bloth hy os:
'Y plegyaf y'n dor hag y fayaf y welen.'

'Below were caverns grim with greedy gloom.'
Lucretia died, aged six years:
'I bow and kiss his rod.'

Geryow Kernewek

Pandra' wren-ny genough,
Agan geryow Kernewek?
A wren-ny donsya genough
Po delynya ikenow,
Leverel dythys fur, rymys-fleghes sempel,
Dysputya gwlasageth py fylosofy?

Prag na scryfa lytherow kerensa – parhap
Moy gref entendys es 'vyth dyscudha?
Nepprys y brederaf oll hemma
Yu sculva termyn ha gwyth:
Rak geryow oll a guth pandra
Ny a vyn leverel yn wyr.

Fatel ytho yllyn-ny gul defnyth
A'gan geryow fol ha whek,
Geryow kerys ha nygromansek,
Geryow gothyk, nep a bon a ves genen-ny?
Syns avan an gweder dh'agan tybyans
'Wheth warnodho, segh-ef glan;
Gesyn dhyn-ny dalleth arta.
Martesen, bledhen war bledhen,
Os arta os, ny a vyth cafos
Worteweth an styr gwyr kellys –
Nag yu yn agan lynow bardhonnek
Mes ynter an lynow-na,
Goskesek, ow hyntya a substans,
Kekemys ny a wayt sygnfya.

Cornish Words

What shall we do with you,
Our Cornish words?
Shall we dance with you
Or portray icons,
Speak wise sayings, simple childish rhymes,
Argue politics or philosophy?

Why not write love letters – perhaps
More intended by them than is revealed?
Sometimes I think all this
Is a waste of time and effort:
For all words disguise what
We truly wish to say.

How then can we use
Our foolish fond words,
Beloved and enchanted words,
Wild words which run away with us?
Hold up the mirror to our thoughts,
Breathe on it, wipe it clean:
Let us begin again.
Perhaps, year after year,
Age after age, we shall find
At last the true lost meaning
Not in our bardic lines,
But between those lines,
Shadowed, hinting at the essence,
Something of what we hope to signify.

Michael Palmer

An Gour Gwedhow Yowynk

Dres termyn hyr, a'm esedh ryb hy horf,
My a wruk perthy cof a'n dedhyow kens,
A'gan demedhyans cot mes bewnans whek,
Ha'n kensa prys y's gwelys, lun a nerth,
Lowen ha whar, mynwharth dh'u dywweus,
Ysyl heblyth, yowynk, splan ha tek.

Mes ty, ow meppyk whek,
Yn cusk, cosel ha tom,
Bys bras ow sugna whath –
Pyth yn dha gever?
Kemerys adhyworthys yu dha vam;
Nefra ny wreth hy aswon,
Tevys dhe os. Y fyth dhys
Bewnans hebthy, flogholeth gwak.
Ny vyth dhys joy, lowena,
Par del wor fleghes erel, my a grys.
Ny wreta clewes nefra corf dha vam,
Medhel ha tom, ow cana hungan dhys,
Ha ty synsys yn close erbyn hy bron.
Nefra ny glewyth spyrys kerensa whek.
Y fyth dhys benen aral, nep mammeth,
Dhe wul an pyth us res dhys, ha namoy.

42

The Young Widower

For a long time, sitting by her body,
I remembered the former days,
Our short marriage but sweet life,
And the first time I saw her, full of strength,
Happy and gentle, a smile to her lips,
Supple limbs, young and bright and beautiful.

But you, my sweet little son,
Sleeping so quiet and warm,
Still sucking your thumb –
What about you?
Your mother is taken from you;
You will never know her
As you grow up. You will have
A life without her, an empty childhood.
You will have no joy or happiness
As other children know.
You will never sense your mother's body,
Soft and warm, singing a lullaby to you,
As you are held close to her breast.
You will never hear the spirit of sweet love.
There will be for you another woman, some fosterer,
To do for you what is necessary, and no more.

William Morris

Nos Gwavek

Lemmyn yu devedhys
An nos, gwavek ha yeyn,
Ha war an rosow ughel
Rew gwyn a-guth an veyn.

Nos dygomol, cosel,
Gans lor arghans, hy yu;
Ha ster pur splan a-lenter
Yn ebren dhorgell-du.

Lyes ur a dewlder
A-vyth kens tarth an jeth,
Pan dhe an howl a-noweth
Ha golow nos a-feth.

Bron y'n gover byghan
A-sy; mes spavenhes
An dowr yu, gans an yey fell,
Cler, boll, a-let y res.

Gwels an ros yu rewys,
Ha'n gwan lorgan a-hel
Goskesow tewl warnedha:
Mes lywyow oll yu kel.

Lyes ur a dewlder
A-vyth kens tarth an jeth,
Pan dhe an howl a-noweth
Ha golow nos a-feth.

Winter Night

Now the night has come,
Wintry and cold,
And on the high moors
White frost covers the rocks.

It is a silent, cloudless night
With a silver moon,
And brilliant stars shine
In a vault-black sky.

Many hours of darkness
There will be before the dawn
When the sun will come again
And light will conquer the night.

Rushes rustle in the stream
But the water is stilled
By the grim, clear, transparent ice
That stops its flow.

The moorland grass is frozen
And the weak moonlight chases
Gloomy shadows across it;
But all colours are concealed.

Many hours of darkness
There will be before the dawn
When the sun will come again
And light will conquer night.

Antony Snell

Travydh Trogh

Hag i ow nesa fin an koes
ow medra tu ha'n golow,
ev a hordhas tromm y droes
erbynn men kudhys garow.

Unn garm lymm a dhassonas
diworth bennow efan brith:
bran unnik a sowdhanas
yn fo mes a skovva'n gwydh.

War an leur ha 'y gorf yn-tenn
parys dhe'n poen a sywyas,
y pys ev: A Dhyw difenn
na vo dhymm ufern brewys.

Y vyrgh vyghan a boenyas
dhodho yn tyegrys yeyn:
toes bleujyow-gwyns a goedhas
mes a'y dorn war dolgh y geyn.

"Ma pythow gweth yn bresel!"
yn hardh yn medh ev dh'y flogh
ow perthi'n gloes yn kosel.
"Nyns eus dhymm travydh trogh."

Dh'y henys ev re dhothya
heb askorn na kroghen vrew.
Bresel – ny's gwelsa nefra:
ass' o revedh porpos Dyw!

Y tienkys an geryow
dre dhel sygh ha skommow gwav
hag ev ow tilea'n dagrow
kyns omhalya hell dh'y sav:

Nothing Broken

As they were nearing the edge of the wood
aiming towards the light,
he suddenly struck his foot
against a rough concealed rock.

A single sharp cry echoed
from broad dappled tree-trunks:
a solitary crow startled,
fleeing the shelter of the trees.

On the ground his body taut
ready for the pain that followed,
he prays: O God forbid
that I should have a broken ankle.

His small daughter ran
to him in a cold terror:
a bunch of wood anenomes
fell from her hand on to his humped back.

"There are worse things in a war!"
he said bravely to his child
bearing the pain calmly.
"I haven't broken anything."

He had arrived at his old age
with neither skin nor bone broken.
War – he had never seen it:
how extraordinary God's purpose was!

The words escaped
through dry leaves and the wreckage of winter
as he wiped away his tears before
slowly heaving himself upright.

"Dha vroder, ev a goedhas
pan drebuchyas ev orth fos:
omsevysi a'n kavas –
yn Iwerdhon hons, yn koes."

An eyl flogh ledhys dre wall,
ha'n vamm dre hir galarow.
Dhodho ev y res heb fall
dh'y gothni durya salow.

Adhiworto y koedhas
bleujyow leyth, krinyon ha ponn.
Yn freth y vyrgh a'n strothas
hy fenn heudh erbynn y vronn.

"Dha golonn – y's klywav kler!"
Ha hi a davas y vogh
"Bydh lowen, a dasik ker:
ty yw salow – travydh trogh!"

"Your brother, he fell
when he stumbled against a wall:
the rebels got him –
over in Ireland, in a wood."

The one child killed by mischance,
and the mother through long mourning.
It was up to him without fail
to endure in a sound state to his old age.

From him there fell
limp flowers, leaf fragments and dust.
Eagerly his daughter hugged him
with her head joyfully against his breast.

"Your heart – I can hear it clearly!"
And she touched him on the cheek.
"Be glad, dear daddy:
you're safe– nothing broken!"

Resek Nos

Hanternos: y poenyas
fol maw gwlys ha ganso morthol
ow kolia tynn peub karr teg
hys agan fordh delyowek.

Dur ha gweder y's gwarias
gans ilewydhieth ahas:
pub boemm kewar a veu gwres
yn musur kepar kompes.

Mar berfyth y obereth
may sywyas taw bras an bedh:
na krenn na kryghya kroglenn,
klys yn pluvek kettep penn.

Gwannhes dre weder dewblek
yn son sogh ha tynkyal hweg
y hwonedhis dhynn an tros
unnsel yn devnydh hunros.

Dydh oer a dhifunas hell
ha howl anyagh ow sevel.
War hy skorenn yn gronn blin
pub edhen stag hy gelvin:
ankoth yn kres mis Ebrel
hwythow ankow a dhehwel.

Sowdhenys an paperwas
a weskis orth pub daras
hag yn unn hokya, yn hos,
y tiskwedhas an terroes.

Lagasow galarus tynn
a blynchyas orth an dewynn:
sugra garow war an grow,
gweder yn rosweyth folsyow.

Night Run

Midnight: there ran
crazy a wild lad with a hammer
sharply wounding each fine car
the length of our leafy road.

Steel and glass, he played them
with cruel musicianship:
each precise blow was made
in a rhythm equally exact.

So perfect his performance
that there ensued the grand silence of the grave:
no stirring nor rippling of a curtain,
snug on a pillow every head.

Attenuated through double glazing
to a dull sound and a sweet tinkling
the noise served us
only as the stuff of a dream.

A bitter cold day awoke sluggishly
with a sickly sun getting up.
On its branch in a soft bundle
each bird with its beak firm shut:
strangely in the middle of April
the blasts of death return.

Astonished the paper-boy
knocked on every door
and hesitatingly, hoarsely,
he pointed out the destruction.

Eyes sorrowful and tense
blinked at the gleam:
coarse sugar on the gravel,
glass in a network of cracks.

Gohelus yn dillas nos
gostyth dhe'gan kevambos
– goelyas kemmynieth difreth –
'dann furvow kentrevogeth
ni a dheuth yn kylgh yeyn:
dadhelva deg mynysenn.

Askus 'vas dhyn o'n oerni
rag diank divlam yn chi
peub dh'y negys privedh ter
plegys orth an pellgowser.

Bashful in night clothes
obedient to our convenant
– a feeble community watch –
in the forms of neighbourliness
we came into a cold circle
for a ten-minute consultation.

A useful excuse for us was the bitter cold
for escaping blameless indoors
each to his urgent private business
hunched over the telephone.

Dy'Goel Felyon Oll 1995

War an woen ughel dann grommnen brav
kala fynni sygh bys kettep fin
fustys ha karthys gans hwythow gwav
kribys leven, gwiver arghans krin.

Benyow eythin dyswrydhyes hager:
bedhlann dhefolys, eskern felsys
ow lytherenna dial euver
ha kovadh norvys diskevelsys.

Ponn safron war an bosow a-bell
ha kennen wyrdh yn krogoes an komm:
keredh dhynn y'gan diskryjyans fell,
gwesyon enyaleth, gwandrysi lomm.

Fyslek yn pryskel unn ahwesydh
ow skoellya ton a-les yn tanow:
debron dynyadow dhe bub prydydh
yn unn gyrghes a'ga hudh y ganow.

Yn gorwel digommol negys gras
fleghes ow kilboesa erbynn tenn
kordennow serf-nija ruth ha glas:
lostow terghys a dhrayl lerghow krenn.

Ma'n howl diveth ow higa'n vywva.
Avorow, yn medh an gwetthavyer,
y tehwel keser lymm ow kisya
mil dyth munys gwrys yn huvelder.

Sentri 'mysk erewi unntrevas:
kowlgarthys kyn fo gans yey ha tan
ny grysir dh'y yeghes bys miras
briallen a'y hordh der eskern bran;

bys blasa'n gluth ha las kynsa'n glaw
bys anella niwl an myttin bludh

All Fools' Day 1995

On the high down beneath a splendid vault
dry tussock straw as far as every limit
threshed and scoured by winter's blasts
combed smooth, wires of brittle silver.

Stumps of furze uprooted, ugly:
a graveyard violated, bones split,
spelling out a pointless vengeance
and remembrance of a world disjointed.

A dusting of saffron on the bushes far off
and a green film on the hanging wood of the combe:
a rebuke for us in our grim disbelief:
servants of desolation, naked wanderers.

Fussing about in a thicket
one skylark scattering abroad a melody sparingly:
an enticing itch for every poet
as he fetches his poems from their hiding place.

On a cloudless horizon the graceful business
of children leaning back against the tug
of cords of kites, red and blue:
wreathing tails drag circling tracks.

The sun is shamelessly teasing the habitat.
Tomorrow, says the pessimist,
returns the sharp hail destroying
a thousand tiny statements made in humility.

A sanctuary amongst acres of monoculture:
although it is wholly cleansed by ice and fire
one won't believe in its health until one looks at
a primrose thrusting through the bones of a crow;

until one tastes the dew and the first sip of rain,
until one breathes the mist of a soft morning

rag surhe aga bos dinamm ha saw:
spavenn munys hwath dhe'n ynys dhruth.

Felyon an norvys kesunyn ni!
Gwren kana dre nosow hir an gwav,
hunrosa dhynn kur hudel dhe'n pri
dhe dhaskorr yeghes dhe diredh klav.

to ensure they are untainted and sound:
once again a tiny respite for the precious island.

Fools of the world let us unite!
Let's sing through the long winter nights,
dream up for ourselves a magic cure for the soil
to restore health to a sick land.

'Medh Hykka

'Medh Hykka... Kows Kernewek
kepar del ves ow karma
war dus enos erbynn gwyns
owth oulya mes a'n gogledh.

Ha my war gamm ow kewsel
a'n eyl tu a weli klys
yn hwistrow der an bluvek:
honn yw myns a'm ownegedh.

Said Dick

Said Dick... Speak Cornish
as if you were shouting
to people over there against a wind
howling out of the north.

And here's me speaking
cautiously from one side of a cosy bed
in whispers through the pillow:
that's the measure of my timidity.

Marghak an Mordardh

An skajynn yowynk a welowgh war an treth
ow kentrynna kowetha hag owth usa gwyls
dre'n prysk spernek y'n ewyn freudhys:
ev a re awen dhe 'n arvedhow freth

a dewlens tont orth an hen dus
y'n treven tewedhek war benn
an als, hag a skwychya 'n groglenn-roes rag golok
a'n gols brith gorm hag owrek na – penn mus,

penn-skav, ow kaboli kedrynn a-varr,
terryas fenestri, dileshyer keun,
noskaner didhynnargh kreg y lev
huder heudhik moen a'n mowesi diswar.

Mes an dus koth krodhek o fest drok-pes,
kildennys yn keginow, an dydh freudhek na.
Mordros taranek, usow glew:
ny welsons fatla veuva uvelhes.

Ha'gan maw ow settya war an nawves tonn,
yn dann ynnia holyoryon war-rag,
an dowr a dewlis sketh a neppyth plos
glan yn y anow. Re'n lonksa ev dison.

War y geyn an gowetha a gronkyas diles.
– Kehys ha'm bys, kepar ha kneus
tanow lows, ha mar nyns ova goemmon
– Dhyw! Didrueth i a wrug anodho ges.

– Nammenowgh ny lenkir an traow ma, devri!
yn medh an medhek ow minhwerthin gwann.
– Marth a'm beus na glywsowgh de
a'n defolans nowydh y'gan dowrow ni.

Trydydh awosa ha'n ebrenn hebaskhes,
mordryk, spavenn varow, taw ankoth.

Knight of the Surf

The young vagabond you used to see on the beach
spurring companions on and shrieking wildly
through the thorny scrub into the tattered foam:
it is he who gave inspiration for the eloquent insults

which they would throw cheekily at the old people
in the weather-beaten houses on the head
of the cliff who twitched the net curtain for a glimpse
of that streaked hair brown and golden – head of a madman.

Scatterbrain, stirring up trouble early,
breaker of windows, unleasher of dogs,
unwelcome seranader with a hoarse voice,
slim joyful encounter of the unwary girls.

But the old carping folk were mightily ill-pleased,
retreated into kitchens, that violent day.
Thunderous surf, piercing shrieks:
they did not see how he was humiliated.

As our lad was attacking the ninth wave,
all the while urging followers forwards,
the water threw a shred of some foul thing
right into his mouth. He had swallowed it straightway.

On his back the friends thumped to no avail.
– As long as my finger, like thin
loose skin, and if it wasn't seaweed
– O God! Pitilessly they made fun of him.

– Not often does one swallow these things, for sure!
said the doctor smiling weakly.
– I'm amazed you didn't hear yesterday
about the new pollution in our waters.

Three days later with the sky now quietened,
low tide, dead calm, strange silence.

Deg glaswas yn glybwisk ha manegow du
a avonsysas didros yn renk a-les.

Yn kompes i a wrug an karth
ow sagha 'n dralyow leyth divlas.
Yn fenestri awartha, minyow koth
a lagattas avlavar awos marth.

Revedh hedhyw yw y fara hwar,
an pollat na, kudynn melen ow tewlhe.
Dhe wir, namna verwis awos tag.
Devos-tremen a glywsowgh bydh y bar?

Ten striplings in wetsuits and black gloves
advanced noisily in rank abreast.

Calmly they did the cleansing
bagging the disgusting wet scraps.
In windows up above, old faces
stared speechless in wonder.

Astonishing today is his gentle demeanour,
that lad, yellow lock turning dark.
It's true he almost died from choking.
A rite of passage, did you ever hear the like of it?

Klappkodh

Klappkodh: klys yn torr ow dorn
didros unn kors drudh;
mes unn lagas ow skwychya
a dest the bolsik abervedh.

Yn dann denna ow haradewder
yn medhav: Mabyar voen yn kosk!
Mes kastus avel pub ydhyn dov
leun a glapp ha kawgh.

Pes henedh y'th esplegyans
a-dhia'n kolommes-karya?
Pan gellsys dha 'gou' hebask
ha dyski gryllya debrenek?

Hebaska dhe vesyas fyslek;
paderow yn hirbedrek hudol:
hunros pub degowek dibowes;
mayn komun dhe nerv keskar.

Nyns eus askus dhe dewel
yn kever neb trufyl ankevys
sians tromm, dout a lelder,
own gowyow, fienasow niwlek.

Mona huswir a dhever
dre wias a woverow nevek,
hys gwarak an kammneves
bys y'n boessa orth y fin:

kaudarn molys konnyk
yn furv kath kwoffys
ow kila adryv minhwarth
a veurgolonn huswir.

Mobile Phone

Mobile phone: snug in the hollow of my hand
silent for one precious moment;
but one eye twitching
is evidence of a little pulse within.

Ever stretching my amiability
I say: Slender chick asleep!
But tricky as any tame bird
full of chatter and shit.

How many generations in your evolution
since the carrier pigeons?
When did you lose your peaceful 'coo'
and learn an irritating chirp?

Solace for fidgety fingers,
prayer-beads in a magic rectangle:
every restless teenager's dream;
means of communion for dispersed nerves.

There is no excuse to keep silent
about some forgotten trifle or other,
sudden whim, doubt about fidelity,
fear of lies, hazy anxiety.

Virtual money trickles
through a web of celestial streams,
all along the arc of the rainbow
right into the pot at its end:

a cauldron artfully moulded
in the form of a satiated cat
receding behind a smile
of virtual magnanimity.

Jori Ansell

Trevas

Ha hwys y dal o,
a'y geyn gloesow
y tug manalow,
    lavur yslann.
Ena ev a wre
godhav klor y vegh;
y fia hware
    heb gonis mann.

Nyns o na fella
Kasor a'n harttha;
'th esa y'n para
    ow trushya ys.
Y koedho dhodho
gul hwel kasadow,
Kyn feu an gweythow
    gwrys gans meur-gris.

Stroth y vryansenn,
kisys der ethenn;
gas-kedhow melyn
    re wodhavsa.
Yth anelli ponn
a wre fustoryon:
y koedhas ev skon
    yn unn basa.

Ev a bethi kov
a'n leys 'bia prov
a berthyans mar dhov
    y'n bel garow
Flerys, podrethek,
an loub fest glusek

66

Harvest

And it was in the sweat of his brow
and the pain of his back
that he brought the sheaves,
    labouring in the cornyard.
There he patiently
suffered his burden,
for he would soon be
    without any work at all.

He was no longer
one of the bravest warriors;
he was in the gang
    threshing corn.
He had to do
the detestable work
although the tasks
    were carried out with great vigour.

His throat was taut,
ravaged by gas,
the yellow mustard gas
    that he had endured.
He was breathing the dust
that the threshers made:
soon he collapsed
    coughing.

He was remembering
the mud that had been the test
of his meek patience
    in the savage struggle.
Stinking, rotting,
the very sticky slime

re's baghsa, 'vel gwyg,
　　An enevow.

Ny via argel
dhe wesyon vedhel
skoellys dre wynsell
　　'vel ysennow.
Yth omladhsens fell,
re wrussens gans nell
Batalyas y'n tell
　　Myttin ha mo.

Ha pan dhehwelsens
pandra a gavsens?
am dus heb revrons
　　orth an vrasyon
Dhiworth Somme ha Mons
alena pan dhothyens
prest dyghtys y vons
　　Avel kethyon.

Aga rewloryon
yn-medh: "Soudoryon!
Tiredh rag brasyon
　　a vydh, dell goedh!"
(An gwiryonedh poes –
Nyns o ragdha klos,
Mes desper ha gloes,
　　ny's tevo goeth).

I re omladhsa
A wlasow a'n brassa
Rydh par may fywa
　　Broyow munys.
'th yskynnsens yn freth
yn-mes drog-sedh,
A ifarn an kleudh
　　an bel tryghys.

that had caught
    the souls like tares.

There would be no refuge
for soft fellows
scattered by a fan
    like grains of corn.
They fought fiercely,
they had battled with strength
in the holes
    in the morning and before the dawn.

And when they had returned
what did they find?
The people had no respect
    for the heroes.
When they came
from the Somme and Mons,
constantly treated
    like slaves.

Their rulers
said: "Soldiers!
There will be land for heroes,
    as is fitting."
(The heavy truth
– there was no glory for them,
but destitution and pain;
    they would have no pride).

They had fought
from the biggest countries
so that the smallest countries
    would be free.
They rose up swiftly
out of the slough,
the hell of the trench,
    the battle won.

Mes ny veu rydhses
rag Keltya or'nys
Saw 'veu dre wonnys
   'Werdhon rydhhes.
Meur a Gernowyon
galsa i y'nn tonn;
dhe vedhow yn gronn
   re gavsens yn gronn.

Dell yw'n parabyl:
an has war'n radell
a wrug y dewlel
   gonador logh.
Skon i a devis:
kyns bos adhvesys
i a omhwelis,
   an bywnans koeg.

Mebyon heb gonis
tramor a woelyas:
an re o gesys,
   dyghtys dignas.
Liv-woeth neb stredh,
a jynn-fustra heydh
a dheuth yn fros freth
   agan ys-has.

"Ogh! Trevas hwerow
o vysyn hedhyw!
Dh'agan teyluyow
   yw mewl truan!
A warva'n jorna
bys vykken pesya?
A allav fia
   a'n nor avlan?

But freedom was not
ordained for Celtia;
but Ireland was set
 free by guns.
Many Cornishmen
had gone into the ground;
in mass graves
 they had found repose.

As it is in the parable:
the seed on the stony ground
had been broadcast
 by a careless sower.
Quickly they grew:
before they had ripened
they collapsed,
 the worthless life.

Lads without work
sailed overseas:
those who were left
 were treated unkindly
Like the flowing current of a stream.
from a barley-threshing machine
flowed a stream
 of our seed-corn.

"What bitter harvest
we are reaping today,
such a disgrace
 for our families!
Will the day
last for ever?
Can I flee
 from the unclean Earth?"

Brian Webb

Ow Avon Splann

Keskan: Ow avon splann, ow avon efan
      ow resek heb lett dhe'n mor,
    ow avon splann, ow avon efan,
      ow treghi dha fordh der an dor.

    An lanwes re lanhas olyow treys an klav'rek
      Ysolt yth esa ow toen;
    dha dhowrow re welas korf ow Myghtern Arthur
      ha'y dhoen dhe gres Avalon.

    Yn goskes dha lanyow y batelyas estrenyon,
      Spanyers erbynn an Frynkyon;
    mes hedhyw y hwelir arwoedh agan bresel
      usi lemmyn war ankor heb son.

    Y'n le mayth omjunya gover Dowr Ythi
      gans dowrow goeth strollek Keynwynn,
    y trehevys ha shapya agan tasow tre vyghan;
      pandr'a wrussons prederi lemmyn?

    Dh'avonyow-maga yw avel derowenn
      gans skorrennow owth ystynna yn-mes
    dhe Ruan, dhe Vylor, Ponsmeur ha Devron,
      mes ow resek eus dha vywnans dhe-ves?

    Dha ganel a dhri ha dannvon pythow;
      sten, glow, ha gwara ha prenn;
    mes an hwelyow a ri dhe'n bobel bywnans
      a'th lenwis ha syger pub den.

My Bright River

Chorus: My bright river, my broad river,
    Flowing incessantly to the sea,
My bright river, my broad river,
    Cutting your way through the earth.

The flood stream has washed the footprints of the leper
    Who was carrying Iseult;
Your waters have seen the body of my King Arthur
    And borne him to the peace of Avalon.

In the shelter of your banks foreigners fought,
    Spaniards against Frenchmen;
But today our battle emblem is seen
    Which is now quietly at anchor.

Where the river Allen mingled with
    The waters of the dirty River Kenwyn,
Our fathers built and formed a little town;
    what would they think today?

Your tributaries are like an oak tree
    With branches stretching out
To Ruan, Mylor, Grampound and Devoran,
    But is your life running away?

Your channel brought and sent riches;
    Tin, coal, merchandise and timber:
But the workplaces that gave life to the people
    Filled you, leaving men idle.

N.J.A. Williams

An Lowarth Cosel [esrann]

Ot yn nans a-hes an hens
sentry sans, corlan kerens
(dyogel argel an lys),
'ter parwysy paradhys.
Ny's anny blyth, brogh na ky;
'ma pays ha powes ynny.
Tek awel y'n tyller taw –
gwan gwyns ha'n gwyth yu glansaw.

Bush ha pren orth pen bloth Cryst
gwedhys yns ha gwedhowdryst.
An ayr yu lym, lom an bar,
'ma pyasen hep kespar.
Keser cales, glybor glaw
a goth hag ergh hag arghlaw.
Rewys mars yu tew ha tyn,
gwreugh slyppya sley war slynklyn.
Cleghy cales cam ny blek
dhe'n alargh (ydhnyk ewlek).
Yn dan orny dor kyn fo
(ass yu yeyn an dreyn adro)
blejan ergh yu serth a'y saf,
dager gwerghgan y'n gwynwaf.
'Ogas gayntwn – gwell dha jer'
yu negys tegen Genver.

★★★

Ny gefys bysquweth y'n bys
le moy fusyk, fortynys
es jarden. Jorna joy ve
may whrug Dew den delynya
hag y'n moyha plesont plas,
yn garthen ges y'n gorras.

74

The Quiet Garden [extract]

Behold in the valley along the pathway
a holy sanctuary, a fold for friends
(secure the retreat of the court),
between the walls of paradise.
No wolf troubles it, badger or dog;
there are tranquility and rest in it –
fair breeze in the quiet place –
weak the wind, and the trees are unshakeable.

Bush and tree at Christ's birthday
are withered and widow-sad.
The air is sharp, bare the twigs,
there is a magpie without a partner.
Hard hail, the wet of rain
falls, and snow and sleet.
Since it is frozen thick and taut,
skate cunningly on a slippery lake.
Hard bent icicles do not please
the swan (a greedy bird).
Although it may be under the bitter cold of the earth
(how cold the thorns are around)
a snowdrop is standing straight up,
a virginal-white tear in the white winter.
'It is nearly spring – be of good cheer'
is the message of the jewel of January.

***

I have never found in the world
a more fortunate, favoured place
than a garden. It was a joyful day
when God designed man
and in the most pleasant place of all,
in an enclosed garden, there placed him.

75

Pan dhe gwaf (govy!) dhe'm gyew
ha my yn anken ancow,
an enef ynnof, tan ef
y'th lowarth, arluth arthnef,
ha'm purra pegh pura gwra
yn gordhyans dhe gerensa.

When winter comes (woe is me!) to my sinews
and I am in mortal agony,
take the soul within me
into your garden, lord of high heaven,
and purify my veriest sin
in the glory of your love.

Ken George

An Velin Goth

Tren a res yn-nes gans nell;
Miryn 'hons a'n pons nep-pell;
Miryn syth an mor y'n Soth,
Gwelyn ni an velin goth,
Pennti ryb an mor, penntir
War lann heylynn heyl Lynnhir,
Le an ke ha kreun ha kons;
Peub a-wel y'n wel a'n pons.
Leun an lynn a'n lanow leun,
Dowr ow krena der an kreun.

Trig re dhe'th, an treth yw bras,
Leys a-les yn le lynn las,
Kreun yw tegys kynth yw teg;
Nyns eus sugal, nyns eus seg,
Gwaneth gwynn na gwaneth du;
Gyllys yns, ellas ha tru!
Nyns eus jynn hedhyw y'n jydh;
Seul a dheffa seuladhydh,
Nyns eus ol war aga lergh.
Ple 'ma'n barlys? Ple 'ma'n kergh?
Bleus a bes bys Breus an Bys;
Spas an velin marnas spys.

Byth pan yllyn ni y'n tren
Mir yn-hons an pons a ren;
Kynth yw an keth gwel ma koth,
Gwelyn hwath an velin goth.

The Old Mill

A train approaches powerfully;
we look some distance yonder from the bridge;
we look directly at the sea in the south,
we see the old mill,
a house by the sea, a headland
on the bank of a creek of the Lynher estuary,
the place of the wall and a pond and a causeway;
all visible in the view from the bridge.
The pond full of the high tide,
water quivering across the pond.

Low tide has come, the beach is large,
extensive mud in place of a blue lake,
a pond which is choked though it is beautiful;
there is no rye, there is no draff,
white wheat nor buckwheat;
they are gone, alas, alas!
There is no machinery today;
whoever might have come formerly,
there is no trace left behind them.
Where is the barley? Where are the oats?
Flour will last until the Judgment of the World;
the lifetime of the mill just ephemeral.

Every time we go in the train,
we give a look yonder from the bridge;
although this same sight is familiar,
we still look at the old mill.

Mester an Porth

A-ugh an grysyow, morer yn y neyth
    a syns y bellgewsigell avel arv;
yma an mester-marner orth y weyth,
    dinamm y dhillas, berr ha gwynn y varv;
tri hylgh a owr a dhiskwedh dhyn y soedh;
    mappow an porth, y wlaskor, yw hewel,
    gwiasenn kevnis owth ystynna pell.
Gwesyon, meghtythyon a herwydh y vodh:
"Gwra lughskeusenna hemma!" Yth yw gwrys;
    ha heb y gummyas ny way gorhel vyth:
mester an soedhva, porth, hag oll y vys.
    Mes my a'n gwel 'vel studhyer seuladhydh,
        ha gonn yn ta: pup dydh an mor a sev
        ha dhiyskynn, yn kosel, hebdho ev.

The Harbour Master

At the top of the stairs, the sea-eagle in his nest
    who holds his mobile phone like a weapon,
the master mariner is at work,
    with spotless clothes, and a short white beard;
three golden bands show us his authority;
    charts of the harbour, his kingdom, are conspicious,
    a spider's web extending far.
Male and female minions go at his bidding.
"Photocopy this!" It is done;
    and without his permission no ship may move;
master of the office, harbour, and his entire world.
    But I see him as a student of former days,
        and I know well: every day the sea rises
        and falls, quietly, without him.

Mick Paynter

Divroans 1890

Ni a wrug mos dhe'n glowek a Dhunelm
rag oberow, govenek, arghans.
Skwettys o yn Kernow agan balyow
akwittys agan ober war-nans.

Devedhys-ni dhe'n bal glow a Goxhoe
ow trovya ena astel ober.
Gwir, kales yw hag ow famya owgh-hwi,
Hag ow famya en-ni, ni a woer.

A vos goddoryon astel ni a skonya,
bywnans yn bal glow ni a vynn.
Ny wren ni pokya tus dhe'n voghosogneth,
res dhe vones dhe ves yw, sowynn.

Mes an bobel a wrug ri boes dhyn-ni;
ha'n tus a wrug ri govonek,
hag yth esa aga bywnans bos omma,
y'n bys a'n wogledh hudhyglek.

Diaspora 1890

We went to the Durham coalfield
for jobs, hope, money.
All skat were our mines in Cornwall
paid off our work down there.

We arrived at the coal-mine at Coxhoe
to find a strike there.
True it's hard when you are starving.
and starving were we, we know.

We scorned being strikebreakers,
life in the coal-mine we wanted.
We will not push people into poverty,
we need to leave here, farewell.

But the people did give food to us;
and the people did give hope,
and our life will be here
in the world of the smoky north.

Ple'ma'an Tus Bras Agan Domhwelans?

Nyns eus neb Ho Chymaen genen,
neb Rosell Luxulyan po Gwlas Ilych Lanyon,
hwath Fydhel Pasko, Barv an Werin,
war agan Avon-ni abervedh neb gorhel,
neb lester brav, agan gwir "Mamm-wynn" ni.
Ernesto Tregavarah, pleth os-ta?

Where Are the Big People of Our Revolution?

There is no Ho Chymayne with us,
no Rosell Luxulyan or Gwlas Ilych Lanyon,
nor yet Fydhel Pasco, the People's Beard,
on our own River aboard some ship,
some fine vessel, our very own "Grandma".
Ernest Tregavarah where are you?

Rag Primo Levi

Dha enev hweg; ha'n bys mar gamm,
ha tamm ha tamm, skrif yn venaghek!
byw yn vinhwerthek, dhe blesya dha vamm!

Trist heb diwedh dha vywnans hir;
euthek yu hwir, rag oll dha furneth
hulla an henedh yw; pyth yw y styr?

For Primo Levi

Your handsome soul; while the world's so bad,
little by little, write monkishly,
live with a smile; to please your mother.

Endlessly sad your long life;
terrible, in truth, for all your wisdom
is posterity's nightmare; what is its meaning?

Gorhel Terrys

Y leveris "Spit dhe'th brath
Namoy, na hwath, nyns ov vy terrys,
Ny wrav vy serrys, po degrena'th parth."

Dhiworth an jydh pan asas ev an dor
Ha dhe Dhulyn mar vrav y teuth an den,
Y spenas ev y vywnans war an mor
Yn lies lester a dreylyas an norvys dien.
War lestrow meur gans aga bagas koynt
A boenyas dhiworth breselyow an bys,
Rag goelya a-dro ha bywa mas yn poynt,
Heb anneth y'ga holonn po sawder y'ga brys;
Yth ombrederis ev, ytho, res o dhodho
Chanjya y vywnans ev awos y vos re goth.
Hag awel hager ma tewlys a-dro
Y teuth mor fell hag y dhenna yn toeth.
An mor, avel menydhyow ughel,
A'n koedhas ena dhe nansow mar dhown,
Y fydh ragdho, martesen, gwithyas, po el,
Dh'y dhri dh'y selwyans a dhiworth Annown.
Our wosa our yth omdewlis an den
Gans yeynder ha ganso an menydh mor.
"My a'th pys, A Dhyw, gav dhymmo vy hepken,
ha my a bass ow bywnans ogas dhe'n arvor."
Ha bys an jydh na pan dheuth ev dhe'n treth, an den,
O spenys war an mor y vywnans oll yn tien.
Dhe dhor sygh pan wrug ev gans troes y dhehwelans,
a-dhia'n jydh na, o trigys gans y fleghes,
          dh'y besya heb hwans.

Gorthel terrys, meur an arnow,
Y'n mor garow. Ha lies budhys,
Unn den a neuv bys dhe'n Arvor Kernow.

A Broken Ship

He said, "Despite your bite,
No more, not again, I'm not broken,
I don't do angry, nor tremble because of you."

Right from the day when he did leave the land
And the man did come to Dublin town so fine,
He spent his whole life on the sea
On many ships that crossed the whole world's span.
Aboard great vessels with their bizarre crews
All running from the struggles of the world
Sailing about, and living in good health,
Without home in heart nor safety in their mind,
It occurred to him he had to get away,
To change his life because he was so old.
While ugly weather there was thrown about,
An evil sea came up and quickly sucked him in.
Like high mountains, the sea
dropped him then into valleys so deep.
There would be for him perhaps a guardian or angel
To bring him back from hell to his salvation.
With coldness and with it the mountain sea
the man wrestled hour after hour,
"Forgive me only God I pray
and I will pass my whole life near the shore."
Until that day when he came to the beach, the man,
Had spent his whole life on the sea.
And from that day when he set his foot on dry land,
Right from that time, he lived with his children
                and continued without need.

A broken ship greatly storm wrecked
In the rough sea. With many drowned
One man is swimming right up to the Cornwall shore.

Bresel Tas

Porthia
Yn medhav vy dhe Gernow dha, farwel.
Yn vro ger na ha genys ha drehevys vy, farwel.
Yn ow dydhyow oll lemmyn pur droblys vy, farwel.
Den a drystyns pur sad, pur droblys vy, farwel.
Dhe Gernow dha yn medhav vy farwel.
Yn medhav vy dhe Gernow dha farwel.

Lucata
Kamm pup-prys nyns yw an vresel
Mes devar pup-prys arloedh fell yw.
Budhogoleth heb klout, ow neuvya vy!
Dyw genen ni, budhogoleth heb klout!
Devar an Arloedh nyns yw fell, ev?
Nyns yw an vresel kamm pupprys.

Napoli
Yndann an voes kynsa penn gwag;
tanbellenn ha'gan honan heb boes,
an aswonnans poes, "Sos!" dewlagas stag.

Anzio
Hag yth esa y'n ebrenn aga jynnow owth omsettya yn krev.
Hag yn tawesek dhe'n benntreth agan lester lowen a dheuth ev.
Spavann y'n vresel a wrug mos an wonnoryon war nans.
Skwith ha pur nownek y hwrug mos an wonnoryon war nans.

Klavgorhel Sen Davydh a wrug kemmeres y gummyas brav
Gans golowys enowys ha krows rudh ha marghogyon glav.
Ha jynn-ebrenn faskor a wrug banna tanbellenn ynno,
ha'n jynn-ebrenn alman yn ayr a wrug arta dehweles dhodho!

Jock Cowie, agan gonner unnik dhe'n arwoedher a skrijas ev,
"Lamm war an pom-pom dhe'n jynn-ebrenn y denna yn mes!"
Distruys y'n ayr an tebel, an vorwesyon lowen ens i.
Gans dowr toemm a vorlu, ha kres, an varnoryon lowen ens i.

Dad's War

St Ives
I say to good old Cornwall now, goodbye.
Born and brought up in that dear land, goodbye,
So troubled now in all my days complete, goodbye.
A man of steady sadness now so very troubled, goodbye.
I'll say goodbye to good old Cornwall now,
To good old Cornwall now I say goodbye.

Lucata
It isn't always wrong, war,
though duty's always a hard master.
Victory without a shot I'm swimming now!
God is with us, victory without a shot!
The Master's duty's sometimes cruel too.
War isn't always wrong.

Naples
Under the table, at first empty handed,
a bomb, and ourselves without food,
the weighty recognition, "Mate!" eyes staring.

Anzio
As the enemy planes were attacking our people in strength from the sky,
and toward the beach-head in silence our happy craft drew nigh,
a lull in the battle gave a chance for our gunners to go below.
Hungry and exhausted our gunners went below.

The Hospital Ship St David in full sight left the shore,
with lights up, with her big red cross, and her wounded of the war.
Then a fascist plane came over and it dropped a bomb on her.
Then the German plane for a second time turned right round in the air.

Jock Cowie, the only gunner left, to the signalman did shout,
"Jump right up on the Pom-Pom, Bunts, and shoot the Jerry down!"
Destroyed in the air the devil was, and the seamen happy they.
With 'sippers all round' and peace, and quiet, the sailors happy they.

Aberfal

Frankedh gwaynys! War ow fennbloedh.
Yn Falmeth koth en vy! Akwitys
yn Kernow keffrys; y'n finwedh a'w bodh.

War'n hynsyow horn hanterkans pols dhe
Stret an Pol, stret koth gans pub sorn,
ha pub kov, pub dorn, ker kolonnow oll!

Falmouth

Freedom won, on my birthday,
I was in old Falmouth! Paid off
and in Cornwall too; at last at my will.

On the railway fifty minutes
to Street an Pol. An old street at every corner,
and every memory, every hand, dear hearts all!

Ha Blair ha Bush

Ha hwi a sywa'gas bodh pupprys,
warlergh 'gas brys yn krev hedhyw.
Nyns yw hygys Dyw. Na vydhowgh tullys
po kekeffrys dall, hwi a vyw
ownek dhe glywes dos pynagol
a dhervynn dhywgh spal an galloes hwi a biw.

Blair and Bush

While you two follow your will always,
and strongly your opinions today.
God is not teased. Don't be deceived
or sometimes blind, you will live afraid
to hear that anyone at all will come
to demand that you forfeit the power you own.

Julyan Holmes

An Taves Hen

Prenn avleythes an ughella gwydh,
kepar dell re dhyn devnydh
pyskador mor, dell wor y fydh
ha sten dell dhastal meur a byth
dhe'n paler, pell a'n golow dydh
y helghyn ni yn men ha menydh,
preydh prydydh a vydh gesys rydh
pub ger a gyffen a'n jevydh,
y dalvos dhyn; pub devynn ha dyth,
dhe'n taves hen ow ri ken besydh
may kewsyn ni yeth nowydh –

kudhys y'n koes
kador ha moes,
yn kokk ha roes
ha payn ha gloes
y'n garrek loes,
y'n kleys ha kloes:
kynth yw y voes;
ha skav ha poes,
settys war droes,
ha kig ha goes,
mar goth ha'n oes!

The Old Language

Heartwood of the tallest trees, hidden in the forest,
provides us with tables and chair;
a fisherman entrusts himself to boat and net
and tin repays many times over the trouble and pain
of a miner, far from the daylight, in the grey rock;
so we hunt, on stone and hill, in ditch and fence.
A poet lets his prey go free, yet it's his meat and drink;
each word we find, significant or commonplace,
has its worth and every saying set back on its feet,
re-christens the old tongue, gives it flesh and blood,
so we speak a new language, as old as the ages.

Kosovo

Diwor' an jydh, war benn dewlin,
an wre'ti, kryghys-oll hy min,
a witha glanyth treudhow chi...
Piw a wra golghi glan an goes
diwor' an nos, ha hi digloes,
hy honan yn hy heudhow hi?
'Glanhes' hy gour ha'y myrghes gwyrgh,
a'y esedh yntra meyn ha'n ergh,
ow pysi Dyw may's daskorro
ha gansa dydhyow kuv Tito!

Kosovo

As dawn broke, a housewife
with a wrinkled face was on her knees,
cleaning the front doorstep...
Who will wash away the blood?
When night falls she is alone in her grief
and her husband and her innocent girls
have been 'cleansed',
sitting between rocks and snow,
praying her God will bring them back –
and with them, the kind days of Tito.

Pawl Dunbar

Bora Mor

Ha'n goelyow leun a wyns yeyn an nos
Ow tythya y'gan lergh ewon gwynn
Le tewl an ebren ha'n bora ow tos
Distowgh yma'n gorwel ow sevel yn tynn.

Ha'n vro yn unn nessa merk tewl a-les
Ha'n gorwel ow treghi hyns ewn ha gwir
Ha'n tonnow owth anella gordhown y'ga blas
Yn-dann rach yw an lynenn wor tu ha'n tir.

Early Morning at Sea

And the sails full of the cold wind of the night
Hissing in our wake white foam
Less dark the heavens and the dawn coming
Suddenly there is the horizon standing sharp.

And the land nearing a dark spread mark
And the vessel cutting a straight and true track
And the waves breathing the smell of the deep
Careful is the course towards the land.

Treth Banna

An tewesva a estyn
Eth mildir po a-dro
Nevra nyns eus havysi lowr
Dh'y lenwel

Tri den a diras
Nans yw pell
A-dro termyn Pask
Heb an arvow ambosys

Owth assaya lettya'n Sevyans
Onyn a veu kemmerys
Kregys ova avel traytour
Pell a'y Vammvro

Yma koven a-ji an tewennow
Hag yn Loundres pell
Kresenn gonisygeth
A dheg y hanow

Duhes o y gov
Yn bresel plontyans an Kledh
Peswar ugans blydhen
Wosa y vernans

Sir Roger Casement a verwis gans onor
Mes ny vynn an Lew Emporieth
Koth, fell, dienorys
Y koth bos gorrys dhe gosk

Banna Strand

The sands extend
Eight miles or about
There are never tourists enough
To fill them.

Three men landed
Long ago
About Easter time
Without the promised arms

Trying to prevent the Rising
One was taken
Hanged he was as a traitor
Far from his Motherland

There is a monument in the sandhills
And in distant London
A Cultural Centre
Bears his name

Blackened was his memory
In the propaganda of the North
Eighty years
After his death

Sir Roger Clement died with honour
But the Imperial Lion will not
Old, cruel, dishonoured
It should be put to sleep.

Ray Chubb

An Als Abarth Cleth

An als abarth cleth
Mar arow mar gref,
Dha enep deantel del yu.
Dhe whythra dha drethow
Tres noth hep eskyjyow
Rag henna yth of vy yn-few.

Dha garrygy mar lywek,
Dha bollennow pystryek.
Py arvor a vyn bos dha bar?
Kyth 'yllyth ta fell bos
Dhymmo vy os ta sos
Pupprys y-th-henwaf ow har.

Ha ny ow-tyskenna
Trulergh war an mena,
Py splander a vyth dhyn hedhyu?
Py buly reveth
A vyth a'ga groweth
Dhe gafos ha gorra yn rew.

Yn pyth yu dha dekter?
Martesen ownekter!
Mar serth ha mar slynkek del os.
Na, nyns yu an dra
A wra dhys mar dha
War drelyans *dha* dekter a bos.

The North Cliff

The north cliff,
So rough and strong:
Your face is dangerous.
It is for searching your beaches,
Barefoot and unshod,
That I live.

Your multi-coloured rocks,
Your bewitching rock pools,
What coastland is your equal?
Although you can be cruel,
You are a comrade to me,
Ever to be named my friend.

As we go down
A footpath on the hillside,
What glory will be ours today?
What strange pebbles
Will be lying
To be found in a row?

In what lies your beauty?
Terror, perhaps,
Since you are so steep and slippery.
No, it is not that
Which makes you so special –
Your beauty lies in changeability.

Graham Sandercock

Chi an Hordh

Gwyns oer krev yma hedhyw
ow tensel tynna a'n barth kledh
nowodhow drog ragos a syw
ha dargan tenkys trist ynwedh.

Na wra ankevi Chi an Hordh
le may triga benyn gans gour hen;
na wra sevel yn ow fordh
– ke yn-mes a'n hyns toeth men.

An bys yw rynnys yn teyr rann –
an koth ha'n gow keffrys ha'n gwir;
war ow chi an howl a splann
ha dres oll an dydhyow hir.

Ty o yowynk, kuv ha hel
mes ny'th o meur a-ji dhe'th penn;
hag y'n eur ma my a wel
y vos kudhys yn-dann lenn.

Na wra synsi dorn a stroth
na wra gortos war an ke;
na wra gasa an fordh goth
po ty a wodhav y'n keth le.

Owth omdewlel gans ansurneth
ow kerdhes mildir kamm;
ow klywes flows, ow kewsel furneth,
geryow freth dinamm.

The House of the Ram

A strong and bitter wind there is today,
biting more keenly from the north;
bad news for you follows
and the forecast of a sad fate too.

Don't forget the House of the Ram,
where a woman lived with an ancient husband;
don't stand in my way –
get out of the way at great speed.

The world is divided into three parts –
the old and the false as well as the true;
on my house the sun shines
and through all the long days.

You were young, kind and generous
but you didn't have much inside your head;
and at this time I see
that it is hidden under a blanket.

Don't hold a hand that squeezes,
don't wait on the hedge;
don't leave the old road
or you will suffer in the same place.

Wrestling with uncertainty,
walking a crooked mile;
hearing nonsnese, speaking wisdom,
fluent perfect words.

Poll Pri

An glaw, an glaw
ow koedha heb powes;
yma den yn poll pri
yn hunros mar dhown;
yn y vrys gwel y vaw
keffrys gwel y vowes
ow koska y'n chi
heb preder, heb own.

Pri gwyn, pri gwynn,
y dhillas yw keglys
a'n gonis mar arow,
mar lyb ha mar boes;
pesya a vynn
yn y ober milligys,
eseli skwith marow
dre'n misyow hir loes.

Dhe-dre orth an oeles
gwreg yowynk ow pobas,
benyn erbysek, diwysek dre nas;
yn kleves, yn yeghes,
ow kwitha hy fleghes,
kales hy bywnans
ha heb gwaytyans bras.

An glaw, an glaw,
kowasow heb lett
ha pri y bal-ober
yw poes gans an dowr;
y ober yw saw
orth an dus ryb an yet
ow hwilas y wober
pub dydh, pub our.

Dhe-dre orth an oeles
gwreg yowynk ow kortos,
benyn dhiwysek, erbysek dre nas;

Clay Pit

The rain, the rain,
falling without pause,
there's a man in a clay work
in such a deep dream;
in his mind a view of his boy,
likewise a view of his girl
sleeping in the house
without anxiety, without fear.

White clay, white clay,
his clothes are bespattered
from the work so rough,
so wet and so heavy;
he will carry on
in his cursed work,
limbs dead tired
through the long grey months.

At home at the hearth,
a young wife baking,
economical, industrious by nature;
in sickness, in health,
protecting her children,
hard her life
and without great hope.

The rain, the rain,
showers without respite,
and the clay of his work shovel
is heavy with water;
his work is safe
from the people at the gate
seeking his wages every day,
and every hour.

At home at the hearth,
a young wife baking,
economical, industrious by nature;

yn kleves, yn yeghes,
ow kwitha hy fleghes,
garow hy bywnans
ha heb gwaytyans bras.

Mar es, pur es
yw mires war-dhelergh
orth oesow tremenys
orth istori an vro;
a via dhe les
dasrosya an troe'lergh
olyow treys genys
yn istori an vro?

in sickness, in health,
protecting her children,
rough her life
and without great hope

So easy, very easy,
it is to look backwards
to past ages,
at the history of the country;
would it be of any use
to retread the footsteps,
footprints born,
in the country's history?

Kataloni

Orth daras igor, ayr a fros,
gwari gwybes rydh yn hes;
gelvin gwennol, kyns an nos,
a dhalghenn skav hy freydhow es;
ha war an ledrow limven loes
my a gerdhas kyns, nyhewer,
menydhyow moel a-ugh an koes
le may trel distowgh an gewer;
my a dhehwel dhis yn skon –
ledrow ledan Rousillon.

Gwinlannow dres an nans a-is,
rew war rew, linennow hir;
sugen du dhe benn an mis
pan dheu an drevas war an tir;
froeth anadhves, hwerow, lymm
a drel yn skon dhe neppyth melys
a vydh pup-prys marthys dhymm,
rin a natur, prest anwelys;
an nos a goedh, an gryll a gan,
kowetha dha, hwarth toemm didhan,
ym syghnans syger katalan.

Pan hedh wor'tiwedh kan an nos,
y koedh kosoleth war an chi;
dhe'm gweli res yw dhymmo mos
ha lemmyn hwans a'm beus anedhi;
er ebrenn efan, tewl ha pell,
hanterwiskys, dillas lows,
kroghenn avel oliv gell,
hi a war dhwelin orth an grows;
my a berth kov gwel ha son;
my a woer pub ger, pub ton,
ha my a dhehwel dhis yn skon –
nosow poeth, hir Rousillon.

Catalonia

At an open door, air streams,
the play of gnats free in a swarm;
a swallow's beak before the night,
seizes nimbly her easy spoils;
and on the grey limestone slopes
I walked before, last night,
bare mountains above the wood,
where the weather changes sunddenly;
I will return to you soon –
wide slopes of Rousillon.

Vineyards over the valley below,
row on row, long lines;
black juice before the end of the month
when the harvest comes on your land;
fruit unripe, bitter, sharp,
will soon change to something sweet
which will always be a marvel to me,
a secret of nature always unseen;
the night falls, a cricket sings,
good company, warm amusing laughter,
in a lazy dry Catalan valley.

When the song of the night finally stops,
there falls a calmness on the house;
to my bed I must go
and now a desire I have for her;
against a wide sky, dark and far,
half-dressed, loose clothing,
skin like brown olives,
she kneels at the cross;
I remember sight and sound;
I know every word, every tune,
and I will return to you soon –
long, hot nights of Rousillon.

Philip Chadwick

Dursonyowdhis

Nevra ny vydh an keth bys arta;
 Ny yllir troesya diwweyth
 Y'n keth gover dowr,
Mes saw roy neppyth hanow –
 Ytho oll yw possybyl
Y'n fantasi kemmyn, perthys yn kov.

Kevys war barchemin po paper y batron
 Yn maner anperfeyth y hanasow berr
Mes diworth bysow passyes, gans gweres a skians,
 Hwath lemmyn y klywyn son lev kler;
Dres an lytherennow: agan styrans gwir.

 Dhyn ni dhe dhrehevel
 Agan gwir agan honan
 Ha skriva war anow
 An termyn a dheu.

God Sound You

Never returns the same world ever
    you cannot step twice
       in the same water-stream
Yet give but a name,
    and all is possible
In the memory's hoard, in the common dream.

Captured on parchment or paper its pattern,
    In imperfect manner its short breaths fleeting,
But from worlds that have passed, with the help of skilled reason
    Still now we hear a clear voice sound,
Beyond the letters, yields our true meaning.

      For us to build
      Our own truth,
        And pen by mouth
        The time to come.

Ervirans Hav

Treweythyow y'n hav
Ha ty a'th esedh,
War dreth po als,
Ha mires war an mor.
Treweythyow y'n hav
Hag yma'n howl ow splanna,
Y teu an tybyans hweg:
Y fydh oll da.

Dres pub kaletter oll,
Dres oll an habadoellya,
Res gans an bysi bys
A bub tydh oll:
Hebaskhes y'n hav,
Y'n kres a'n jydh mar goskek,
Y'n toemmder dha gorf:
Unn wodhvos ewn sertan.

Treweythyow y'n hav,
Ow mires orth an vlydhen,
Y'n lagas dha vrys,
Kynyav ow tos yn skon:
Treweythyow y'n hav,
Dhe wul neppyth mar vyghan,
Ervira a wredh martesen...
Mes henn, ow flogh, a dhegoedh dhis.

Treweythyow y'n hav,
Ty a woer dha vos kevrennek:
Bennigys osta rann
A Natur ha hi kuv.

Summer's Resolution

Sometimes in summer
When you are sitting
On beach or cliff
And gazing on the sea.
Sometimes in summer
And when the sun is shining
There comes the notion sweet
All will be well.

Beyond every hardship
Beyond the clamour
Sent by the busy world
Of everyday
Becalmed in summer
At the sleepy day's midpoint,
In the warmth of your body:
One true knowledge ascertained.

Sometimes in summer
The year you are reviewing
In the eye of your mind
With autumn coming soon:
Sometimes in summer
Perhaps you decide
To do something so little...
But then, my child, it's right for you.

Sometimes in summer,
You know you are connected:
A blessed part of Nature
Who is kind.

Tim Saunders

An Pennlanw

(54vz Pedhyzlu Maesow Chassya dhÿ Dhin Wagner, Trev Jarl, Karolynedh Dhyghow, Gwortheren 18ez, 1863)

Du ydh o tonnow'nn lanwez
a-hyz ann gworwel ha'y lez,
gwynn ann traeth kul may y'ponsonz
a-dreus lestow feuz ha' chonz,
kann ann kribow durewynn
ma y'c'hwevre mîl vizeug ynn,
rudh ann pennlanw hoarnlomm,
mordrosow trenkvog ha' plomm.

Flÿc'hez hen Daz ann Dowrow,
meibyon Iweredh heb gwow,
yn-tdÿnythyz ganz gwaityanz
yn-ghenyz worth sorr mar sanz:
rÿ'dhothyenz kämm ha' mïlgâmm
dhÿ wolc'hi dhÿ-vaes ann namm
c'hwath a blose'nn gÿsterenn
a-warthev war ann las nenn.
Skianz breic'h ha' nerth ympynn
a'gÿmmere dalghenn tynn
worth dywedh yn karn kledhydh
herwydh gwir ann kazor rydh:
â pywen bÿz yn mîlvloedh
ny'welen byth skoedh worth skoedh
dre'nn oesow pell hag arav
vertu mar gadarn a y sav.

Y'savsonz polz y'nn gworor
yntre'nn tiredh kaeth ha'nn mor
ha' saluzi'nn howl owrdhrudh
a nell aga gwythi rudh:
ÿna'n-jolyv hag antrenk

118

The High Tide

(The 54th Massachusetts Infantry at Fort Wagner, Charleston, South Carolina, 18 July 1863)

Black were the waves of the tide
the length and breadth of the horizon,
white the narrow beach where
they ran over barriers of fate and chance,
shining white the crests of steel foam
where a thousand slender bayonets glistened,
red the iron-bare high tide,
billows of sour smoke and lead.

The children of the ancient Father of Waters,
in truth the sons of the Atlantic,
begotten by hope,
born to so holy an anger:
they had come step by thousand steps
to wash away the stain
that still befouled the constellation on the blue above.
It was the knowledge of arm
and the strength of brain
that would take a taut grasp at last
on the hilt of a sword
according to the right of a free warrior:
if I lived to be a thousand years old I should never see
shoulder to shoulder,
through the long and slow ages
such mighty manhood making its stand.

They stood for a moment in the marshes
between the enslaved dry land and the sea,
and saluted the gold-previous sun
with the vigour of their red veins:
then, lively and without bitterness,

ydh enragsonz renk ha' renk,
musurdoth yn peub dywdroez,
bywgarenzedh yn peub gwoez.
Y'nn dÿc'hes war ann ammug,
dowdothya'n skôn i a'wrug
ganz nell froz dhulas avon
yn-un ÿmmsettya a-bon,
glas sewt aga dynyteth
heb namm, heb miken, heb meth,
triliw aga banerow
a-uc'h ann tyweuz ha'nn grow.
Yn fysk ha' froth ha' festin
y'tardhsonz war wal ann dhin,
taranow y'ga bannlev
yn-un dhÿglena leur Nev:
yn-despyt dhÿ vyrdh belenn
dre vreic'h, dre golonn, dre benn,
war-yow ann lu a rezas
dhÿ skattya ann gworthrec'h kas
ganz mall dre'nn skeuzow mogdywl,
divlanna dhÿ'nn nos ha'nn nywl.

Pan sevys ann howl ternos
a-uc'h koezwig, traeth ha' ros,
war lergh ann ladhva dhirveur
ydh yze hanter war-leur:
yn-tont a-uc'h ann gworthvur
y'tdonzye, yn-stryg ha' sur,
baner growseug ann eskar
yn mysk ann awelow c'hwar:
heb revronz, aga thÿwylyl
y'ghwrug ann eskar mar vyl
avél atl dhÿ hirgleudh
rag dispres, rag meth, rag keudh,
yn gwaityanz tÿrri spyryz
ann gwir glan er bynn ann byz.

Mez ow' profya mîl dhispres
ny'wrug ann eskar y les,
lemen tynna aer ebrenn

they advanced rank by rank,
a measured speed in each pair of feet,
love of life in each one's blood.
In the charge on the defences,
they quickly doubled their pace
with the energy of a dark blue river
as they attacked at a run,
blue the livery of their dignity,
without stain, without spite, without shame,
the three colours of their flags
above the sand and the gravel.
In rush and turmoil and haste
they burst on the outer defences of the fort,
thunder is their cheer
shaking the floor of Heaven:
despite ten thousand bullets
through arm, through heart, through head,
on ran the host
to smite the hateful oppression
eagerly through the smoke-dark shadows,
disappearing into the night and the fog.

When the sun rose
the next day above the forest,
beach and heath after the enormous slaughter,
half were laid low:
arrogantly above the rampart
there danced, sprightly and assured,
the cross-flag of the enemy
amongst the gentle breezes;
without respect, the enemy threw
them so vilely like rubbish
into a long ditch for insult,
for shame, for affliction,
in hope of breaking the spirit
of that bright truth against the world.

But in offering a thousand insults,
the enemy did not do his own good,
but rather drew the air of the sky

yn korrwynz tynn war y benn:
frankedh c'hweg yn enawel
a'c'hwavas dre braz ha' gwêl,
fudha peub kae ha' dowrlann,
yn vertu gwlyc'hi peub gwann.

Tryg rÿ'vu tro, war rydhzyz,
rÿ'dovas c'hwynn trenk y'nn yz,
howl rÿ'sevys ha' sudhaz,
kres rÿz askoras kanz kaz,
mez ot lanwez dhidhifyg,
ÿmmc'hwydh mor arta na'dryg,
rei ow' sudhaz dhÿ'nn twyeuz
a'fethas peub hagr feuz:
rudh ann pennlanw hoarnlomm,
mordrosow trenkvog ha' plomm,
kann ann kribow dur ewynn
ma y'c'hwevre mîl vizeug ynn,
gwynn ann traeth kul ma y'ponsonz
a-dreus lestow feuz ha' chonz,
du ydh o tonnow'nn lanwez
a-hyz ann gworwel ha'y lez.

in a crushing whirlwind on his head,
sweet freedom as a storm
blew through meadow and field,
overflowed every hedge and bayou,
steeping all the weak in manhood.

There has been, at times, an ebb of freedom,
sour weeds have grown in the corn,
the sun has risen and set,
peace has brought forth a hundred battles,
but this is an inexhaustible tide,
the swelling of a sea that will not ebb again,
men who by sinking to the sand
overcame every vicious fate:
red the iron-bare high tide,
billows of sour smoke and lead,
shining white crests of steel foam
where a thousand slender bayonets glistened,
white the narrow beach where they ran
over barriers of fate and chance,
black were the waves of the tide
the length and breadth of the horizon.

Tavow

Ot omma dhÿz gwlazgarenzedh
    ann losow,
       emprwreth allozeug
          ann c'hwynn ha'nn spedhez!
Ryb agan kaeow
    a-dreiv agan chÿow,
       hag yn mysk agan paelow dov
         y'ma nerth gwylz
           ann planzow;
luyow ledan bêst
    a'vynn dÿc'hesi war agan toyow,
    dalghenna y'gan muryow,
    ha' potya aga deinz.
Y'ma danjer dhÿn diwreidhya
    ha' kowllÿski
       ann planzow,
gwul dhÿdhy gwodhevyl
    dirloesow muskog
       yntre'gan deinz ni.
Dÿnarc'h y'gan bydh
    arteithya ha' lÿski,
       trÿc'hi ha' moldra,
         dÿstrewi –
ha' woze ann aerva,
    ann hagr blanzow
       a'vynn liva a-dreuson ni
    ha'gan treilya
       dhÿ'nn dhoar arta.

Touches

Here you have the patriotism
 of the vegetables,
  the powerful empire of
   the weeds and the brambles!
By our hedges,
 behind our houses,
  and amongst our tame fences,
  is the wild strength
    of the plants,
broad armies of moss
 that will charge at our roofs,
  seize our walls,
   and kick their teeth.
We have the jurisdiction to uproot
 and entirely to burn
  the plants,
make them suffer
 mad agonies
  between our teeth.
We shall be welcome
 to torture and burn,
  cull and murder,
   exterminate –
 and after the battle,
  the bloody plants
   will flow over us
  and turn us
   to earth again.

Awedh [esrann]

Rialto
A-dro dhÿ stumm y'nn kammheil
an skath y'nn eur'mma a'dreil,
hag ot a-dreus ann Ganel
ponz ewnblyg stowt y'gan gwel,
fenestrow y'ga hunroz
a gÿnwerth a-uc'h ann froz.
War-nug y'ghwoen heb gwovynn
py skeuz rÿ'dheith er y bynn,
ponz rÿ'n troezse musurgows
yn foedhwe ha' hir a bows,
yn kryc'hvand, gwamm, ha' kledhydh,
uc'havonzyanz, ha' sorr rydh.
Gwas a'nn ryz war ann avon
a'nn ponz 'mma a'glywas son,
gwea gwaraeow frenndhoes
rag didhana tuz y oes,
aga gwel a'ga honen
yn roth tuz oes ha' bro gen.
Dyn a'hunrozy ankow
a'holyas ann skathow kow
rÿi serc'h dhÿ vaw pennvelynn
ha'y gara a garanz tynn,
skullya kneuz noeth y golonn
war eneb diÿmmglyw tonn:
Dyn rÿ'skwithse a vywnanz
a'dhaeth omma yn-leun c'hwanz
gwordhyanz ha' kloz ha' bysmer,
chonz dilesyl peub tra ger,
gwelez pÿrthi y alar
yn eneb gwovizus kar,
c'hwanza ha' helghya'nn kowal
a-hyz ann ynnhynzi sal.
Hag omma, tro, yowynkor
a'vywy'n-honz dhÿ beub or
a'dhalghennas yn pynzell
rag trewana preidh y sell
war arenebow gwastaz

Watercourse [extract]

High Bank

Around a bend in the curved estuary
our boat now turns voluntarily.
Across where the wide channel becomes tight
a straight-bend bridge comes into our sight.
Its splendid ornate windows hold a dream
of commerce conducted above the stream.
Immediately I knew without asking
in which chosen shadow I was basking.
The bridge that measured speech had tradition:
lengthy dresses, and lace in addition,
fancy ruffs, tight doublet and sharp sword too.
Here ambition and anger one could view.
One time, a fellow from a river's ford
heard tell of this bridge's dramatic horde,
and wove exciting plays upon the page
to entertain the people of his Age.
Their view of themselves was transformed right here
to the shape of another Age's sphere.
There's the tale of a man who dreamt death
and followed the hollow boats' shibboleth.
He even gave love to a fair-haired boy
and daily loved him long and with great joy.
Then he spilled the naked flesh of his heart
on the unfeeling face of a wave's art,
and a man who had long tired of life
came here full of desire's yearn and strife
for humiliation, glory and praise,
a chance to abandon all former days
and see his own pain borne and newly lend
in the anxious face of a goodly friend.
There is desire to pursue the whole
'long the salty paths of the river's roll.
Here once, a young man with brush, like a wand
who had every border lived beyond,
came and grabbed hold of a new painting truss,
so as then to capture his prey's gaze thus:
on flat canvas he painted pictures great,

127

avél frwythow yr war blaz
yn-leith a dhownder lannerc'h,
i lowr rag difuna serc'h
yn neb a'wel polz senzyz
yn spavenn hedra vo'nn byz.
Sawor heli ha' gwlybvaen,
glastethez, ha' pyskez braen,
skubyon kynz byw dyw varghaz,
drudh tro mez nâ mwy a vaz
a'm drÿ yn-tro dhÿ haneth
hag yn hy thynnwe a'm pleth.
Tros jin a'lergh kolonnlamm
a-hyz awedh dromm a gamm:
a-dreiv dywvalvenn spavel
y'ghwendryth a-vaes a'w gwel.
Agan kÿweith a'vinc'hwardh
tu ha' ty yn un rÿi dardh:
y'n medh êv: "Penn ann trummaj
skwitha y'n gwra, dervynn raj.
Mann pell lêmmyn ann tremmen
dhÿwc'h chwi, y'n lighav yn-len,
ogas dhÿ golonn lammsal
agan kaer yn hy hun ral.
Dhÿ bennwedhow kanz ynys
yn dydhyow an gwoez ha'nn c'hwys
y'foas tuz ann gwastattir,
yn-un c'hwi'laz argel gwir
a-vaes a dhrehaedh argaz,
a dhalghenn gworthrec'h ha' braz,
Maes a dhorn, tro, y'c'hwilsonz
nertha feuz ha' kryffei chonz
a'ga pharth aga honen
ow' setttya kadarnow gren
omma war ann Lann Uc'hel,
treilya gwern dhÿ blen a wel.
"Rag hÿnna sur," y'n medhav,
"omma nynz yz derow brav
agas kaer gadhleug vrentin
lemen yn-maes worth hy fin."
"Gwir dhâ eir: worth ann ammal,

128

fine 'Still Lives' and fresh fruits upon a plate
that seemed still moist from the depths of a glade.
They were to awaken love ready made
in whoever saw them for a moment,
in long lulls by the present world sent.
There is a smell though of brine and wet stones,
decaying vegetables and fish bones.
This is the rubbish of the two markets,
valuable once, but now in thrown packets.
The foul odour brings me back to this night
and slowly weaves me into a plait tight.
The noise of the engine tracks my heartbeat
bent beside a suddenly curving leat.
Behind my two eyelids, tired and beat
you soon wander out of my sight's conceit.
Our comrade smiles towards you instead
giving an inclination of his head.
He says, "At the end of all voyages you fare,
when you become tired, you must take care.
Not far now, the passage for both of you –
madam, I swear it loyally and true.
We are very near the salt-beating heart
of the sleeping city's most central part.
Though it was to the islands, I must say
that the people once fled, back in the day
of war and hate, of red blood and hot sweat.
That's where the plains-people a retreat set
On there, they were out of invasion's reach,
avoiding oppression's betraying speech.
Later on, their war they sought to enhance
by giving new strength to fate and to chance,
so they all worked for their own safety's sake,
placing high barricades beside the lake,
and right here, they worked upon the High Bank,
turning marsh to land, so the waters shrank."
"I certainly believe all that," I say.
"This isn't where bravery was in play –
here on the High Bank's elevated ledge,
but rather – away out there, at her edge."
"Yes, you speak the truth. The edge was the place

yn mysk ann tewennow sal,
ann fynnwelz ha'nn gwylaneuz,
y'ghworrsoz seil agan feuz.
Dhÿ duz kwrr ydh on henath,
ÿna y'ma ann gwreidh a'hwath.
Tamm ha' tamm i a'dhyskas
gwul ewn yntre gwas ha 'gwas,
trokkya ann frwyth ha'nn denar,
krefni gwylz, gwoveneg c'hwar,
trokkya hudh er bynn jorneth,
gwertha eur ha' prena seth,
gwertha polzow rag aval,
gwertha c'hwys, prena nerth gal.
Bÿz yn kolonn ann syteth
gworc'holyon a'dhoe heb meth,
yn-poes a gÿvaoeth kibyyz
a bezwar bann pella'nn byz,
gwara byw karg heb revronz
a'nn arvor evan yn-honz.
Yn kreis ann vorva evan
y'settsonz oelez ha'tan
ma y'skapsonz tiredh difyc'h,
derai hag eudh ann tir syc'h.

130

amongst the salty dunes, the island's space,
where the berrygrass and seagull's prate
were the true foundations of our fate.
We're progeny of this fringe domain, see,
and rooted there always: ingrained are we.
Little by little they learned to make good
and do right in each fellow's neighbourhood.
They could soon exchange fruit for a penny
and let go greed; gave courtesy money.
One could swap merriment for a day's work.
Sell an hour: have a pot as a perk.
For the bite of an apple, sell your might,
and swap your sweat for a criminal's plight.
All this became the heart of the city.
Shameless ships found here a new sanctity.
They were filled with snatched financial health,
from all four corners of the world's wealth.
They lived a cargoed life without respect,
from beyond the wide coasts that went unchecked.
In the middle of the salt marsh so broad
they placed both hearth and fire for their horde.
From devastated land, they could escape
away from the terror of dry land's shape."

Translated by Alan M. Kent

An Ros Du

Pyu a bew an beth y'n ros,
hep hanow, hep men, hep fos,
deu vyl seson ow cortos?

Pyu a bew beth pen an hens
may can hen govow y'n gwyns?
Ruth y fu gwels arak kens.

Pyu a bew an beth y'n knogh?
Pan drelyr lagas dh'y logh,
Gwreth colon a vyth pondrogh.

Blackheath

Whose is the grave in the heath,
without name, without stone, without wall,
waiting two thousand seasons?

Whose is the grave at the end of the road
where ancient memories sing in the wind?
Grass was once red.

Whose is the grave in the mound?
When eye is turned into lake,
heart's roots are cut by pain.

Gol Snag Bud

Scor y's can
rythsys ha'y resyas velan,
fruthow coynet ha fren cruel,
fler knes, ha blejyow bluth glan.

Ger dre gos,
lavar dre lanergh dor-os,
galw dhe gevrang gulgel,
lef gwyrth ow lywa bys los.

Mor ha mes,
lun a levow ha tonbrays,
a wolow a wy gorwel,
brynten fest ha bras hag es.

      Dhe'n gevrang yn an bush a frysk,
    huth y'ga mysk, pup cam dhe'n dref wyn
      ma y tassen kerghyn a woslam a lesk.

Bude Jazz Festival

It is branches that sing
freedom and its blues rhythm,
strange fruit and cruel excitement,
stench of flesh, and soft bright flowers.

A word through a wood,
speech through a clearing as old as the earth,
a call to a slender secret shire,
a green voice colouring a grey world.

Sea and field,
full of voices and of wave applause,
of light weaving a horizon,
most noble and big and easy.

    To the narrow shire the crowd will hasten,
  with merriment amongst them, every step to the fair town
      where the surrounds echo with a burning pulse of blood.

An Edenva

Y'n jeth kensa my a vyn
formya'n Nor yn keynvys gwyn.

Gwels ha blejan ha pren glas,
ebren dhown ha dowrow bas:
pren glas ha blejan ha gwyns,
dowrow bas hep forth na hens.

Whethennow ow synsy bes,
y les ha y dhownder ha'y hes:
synsy an bes war balf ow dorn,
hes ha les a len'w pup sorn.

Y'n jeth kensa my a vyn
dha formya a'n pry clor gwyn.

The Eden Project

In the first day I will
create the Earth in a white universe.

Grass and flower and green tree,
deep sky and shallow waters:
green tree and flower and wind,
shallow waters without way or path.

Bubbles holding a world,
its breadth, its depth and its length:
holding the world on the palm of my hand,
length and breadth will fill up every cranny.

In the first day I will
create you from the cool white clay.

Judith Larham

Pysadow rag an Naw Kans

Tas, puptra yw ow herensa –
Teg, bras, ow pesya.
Gwir, ow toemmhe, krev, ow fetha.
Ow harer vy a'm karas.

My a worwedhas gans ow harer
Yn gwel Kernewek,
Yn-dann an howl, yn-dann an ster,
Dew gorf, ow tava, yn kerensa.
Bywnans a-derdro dhyn, bywnans ynnon,
Bywnans nowydh y'm torr.

Tas, ow harer a sorras – ragos tejy.
Tas, ow harer a geskerdhas dhe-ves – ragos tejy.
Tas, yn-medh vy 'Dyw genes' dhe'm karer – ragos tejy.

Kokow gwag y'n porth a wortas,
Balyow tawesek ha du a wortas,
Benynes ha kothmans a ammethas
Enyvales ha parkow – oll ow kortos.

Torrow gwag yn Karesk a wortas,
Mebyon a Gernow engrys a wortas,
Soudoryon astranj gans arvow a wortas,
A wortas an ober den a Dhyw.

Lemmyn ow harer a worwedh
Yn gwel estren,
Ow harer a worwedh yn lonk goes,
Yn-dann an howl, yn-dann an ster,
Naw kans korf, ow tava.
Mernans a-derdro ev, mernans ynno ev,
Mernans y'm enev.

138

Prayer for the Nine Hundred

Father, my love is everything –
Beautiful, large, lasting,
True, warming, strong, conquering.
My love loved me.

I lay with my love
In a Cornish field,
Under the sun, under the stars,
Two bodies, touching, lovingly.
Life all around us, life in us,
New life in my belly.

Father, my love became angry – for you.
Father, my love marched away – for you.
Father, I said 'goodbye' to my love – for you.

Empty fishing boats in the harbour waited,
Silent, black mines waited,
Women and old men farmed
Animals and fields – all waiting.

Empty bellies in Exeter waited,
Angered sons of Cornwall waited,
Foreign soldiers with weapons waited,
Waited for the work of a man of God.

Now my loves lies
In a foreign field,
My loves lies in a bloody gully,
Under the sun, under the stars,
Nine hundred bodies, touching
Death all around him, death in him,
Death in my soul.

Y'm taves kernewek vy difennys,
My a'th pys:

Tas, byrl dhis ow harer
Ha'y naw kans broder;
Tas, gwra ow sostena
Ha'm naw kans hwoer;

Tas, ow flogh angenys gwra soena,
Hag oll an fleghes an vro ma,
Ynwedh – rag peub a'n naw kans –
Ro dha gummyas dh'aga diala.

In my forbidden Cornish language,
I beseech you.

Father, embrace my love
And his nine hundred brothers;
Father, sustain me
And my nine hundred sisters;

Father, bless my unborn child,
And all the children of this country,
And permit them to avenge
Each of the nine hundred.

Neil Kennedy

Try Flam a Dan

Kensa flam en tolgow ha me wellas e doola,
sendgi papyriow ter besias whanjak.
Nessa flam colowi ha me wellas lagadgow,
terlentri en noz, du ha sianjak.
Tridga flam annowi ha me wellas e ganow,
sendgi an purvan ter gwessiow crownik,
en crez an noz younk na,
ha ny kelles en cooz.

Three Flames of Fire

A first flame in the darkness and I saw her hands
holding papers between eager fingers.
The next flame flaring and I saw eyes
shining in the night, dark and capricious.
A third flame lighting and I saw her mouth,
holding the spliff between full lips,
in the middle of that young night
when we were lost in the wood.

An Vlewan Looz

Ha ny a kerras war wolas an moar dha drig,
me wellas drera dhez bes edn vlewan,
na moy vel onen mesk an rooz,
apert ha spladn o trellies looz,
ha chy dhom colan adhysompyas
me oya sur dreram cara che.

Ha perthi co gon promas pell ve gwres,
me venja abma dhez ha gudhvas mar vo crees
pe rama doaz war hez adro dha che.
Vedh termen nenna trellia looz warbar?

The Grey Hair

As we were walking on the bottom of the sea at low tide
I saw you had a hair,
just one amongst the red,
clear and obvious that had gone grey,
and all at once in my heart
I knew I loved you.

And remembering our promise made long ago,
I wanted to kiss you and know if there'll be peace
when I finally come back to you.
Will we have chance to go grey together?

Meriasek

Marners, darsona dhewh,
mars ewh da Vreten.
Mar menno moaz da moar
adhor an metten,
mall ew gena ve moaz,
et agoz lesster geno.

An gwins dha cors,
gon lesster leal senji.
Gero ny oll dha'n
lovonow gansenji,
Ha tedna 'man an gool,
mates ve, gen colan.

Lebmen an Chanel ew,
gena ny tremenes.
An gorhal ny dha'n kay,
per wir ew kelmes,
deaw vaner gwidn ha du,
gwidn ha deaw a neija.

Meriasek

Sailors, God bless you,
if you're going to Brittany.
If you'll put to sea
in the morning.
I'd love to go with you
in your ship.

May the wind hold fast
to our ship's course.
Let us all
grab hold of the ropes
and haul up the sail
mates heartily.

Now we've
crossed the Channel.
Our ship is safely
made fast to the quay,
Two black and white flags,
black and white flying.

Brilli a Clappia

Brilli a clappia, gerriow fir, brabm an gath,
Silly a neija, losiow hir, brabm an nath,
Kenkras a moaz da gova dadn,
Gubman ha hugez billy kern.

Pandra ew hedna? Crogan laz, lagas rooz.
Emava tedna, scogan mez, tabm booz.
Deaw baw derakta terri, trehi,
Ganow ageri, tebri kig.

Legest ethewa ! Mava toaz, eball stowt,
Onen an brossa, ethik brauz, nag ez dowt.
Ema an bivin boovin groovin'
Cuntel an browian dhor e li.

Mackerel Talking

Mackerel talking, wise words, nonsense,
Eels swimming, long tails
Crabs going to hide under
seeweed and great round boulders.

What's that? Blue shell, red eye.
It's pulling a mackerel's head, a bite to eat.
Two paws in front of it breaking, cutting,
Mouth open, eating flesh.

It's a lobster! It's coming, a rough character,
One of the biggest, awful big, no doubt about it.
The prawns are groovin'
Gleaning crumbs from its breakfast.

An Brennik

Gero ny meras ort an brennik.
Stag enz ort an garrak,
Ke vo hy gwasges.
Noth ha garow go theller tythy,
Yen ha hollanak.

Otowns glena ort an aulz dowedhak.
Stowt enz ha kelednak.
Senji an carn pilles;
Serra ev lez anjy a verew,
Crev ha sevylliak.

Mowns dirria andelha bedn moar ha hagar-awel;
Nag ez keingen, na todn, na whath froz,
a ell go lowsal a go leah cumpas,
Obma lebma'n tir eria bedn an moar.

Rabo spannel dha ny mala ny seweni vel an brennik,
Tabm calmindgy, awel vaz,
Rag obma me am bedh chy dre voma bew,
Scath rag an puscas ha looar rag an losow.

Nag era ny war an doar,
na whath war voar,
bes thera ny trega ter an deaw,
lebma'n tir a codha en moar,
lebma'n bressel visquethak dirria,
ter an doar seh ha'n dowr gleb.
Gero ny gwitha gon leah cumpas,
Ga peneek vel an brennik.

The Limpets

Let's look at the limpets,
They're fast to the rock,
though battered.
Naked and rough their rightful place,
Cold and salty.

Behold them clinging to the battered coast.
Steadfast and bold,
holding the stripped rock;
Clenched to it so they don't die,
Strong and unmoving.

So they last against sea and storm.
There's no swell, nor wave, nor stream even,
that can loose them from their fit place,
here where the land resists the sea.

May we have still water to thrive like the limpets,
a bit of calm, fair weather,
for here I'll have a house as long as I live,
a boat for fish and a garden.

We aren't on the land,
nor yet the sea,
but we're between the two,
where the land falls into the sea,
where the everlasting war goes on,
between the dry land and the wet water.
Let's stand fast,
as unyielding as the limpets.

Baner Vith

Nag ez fowt dem a vaner,
Na vern pe liu,
na crowz na steran na gwarak.
Ruth, gwidn ha glaz na gwidn ha du.
Na ro ve oy rag hedna.

Nag ez oathom a vaner,
Queth war predn.
Me venja kens an goolan,
Looez e gil ha gwiden e vrodn,
neija heb gwern en ebarn.

No Flag

I don't want a flag,
whatever colour,
nor cross nor star nor crescent.
Red, white and blue nor black and white.
I don't care an egg about that.

There's no need for a flag,
a rag on a stick.
I prefer the gull,
grey backed and white breasted,
flying in the sky without a mast.

Cliff Stephens

Kryjyans Nowydh

Yma Pow Sows ow kyni mernans unn bennseviges,
Ytho res yw dhyn kyni ynwedh,
Rag an gyns-wreg a dhug angaradow
Neb a usyas arghans kernewek
Dhe be kost y dorrva demmedhyans.
Mernans trist, heb dhout,
Mes an gorvuskogneth
Gwrys gans an wask
A wra gwruthyl henhwedhel a sanses
Avel mamm Grist.
Dineythyans kryjyans nowydh,
Perfeyth yw hi, dres keredh,
Kolonnoges ha mertheres
Salwadores, yn hwir,
Le pergherinses yw hy bedh
Rag an gryjygyon wir.
Diworth an bedh
Hi a yll yaghhe an glevyon,
Pysewgh, ha yaghhes a vydhowgh.
Pysewgh war'n Dhywes Veur
A gerensa ha kres,
Ha'n gorughelder a Bow Sows.

A New Religion

England mourns the death of a princess,
And so, we must mourn too,
For the ex-wife of an uncaring duke
Who used Cornish money
To pay for his divorce settlement.
A tragic death, without doubt,
But the mass hysteria
Generated by the press
Creates the legend of a saint-like figure
To rival the mother of Christ.
The birth of a new religion,
She is perfect, beyond reproach,
A heroine and martyr,
A female messiah, no less,
Her tomb a place of pilgrimage
For the true believers.
From the grave
She can heal the sick,
Just pray and you'll be cured.
Pray to the Great Goddess
Of love and peace
And English supremacy.

Gorhel an Gethyon

Gorhel kethyon a woel diworth an brastir tewl
Gans karg a dus rag aga gwertha
Avel kig un norvys nowydh.
Alhwedhys yn torr an gorhel
Chaynys warbarth y'n tewlder
Hag ow taga y'n ayr flerys
Ownek ha serrys.
Benynes ha fleghes ravnys gan an meni,
An re varow tewlys y'n mor rag skavhe an karg.
Wel, niggers yns i,
Nyns yns tus yn hwir.

Y'n dydhyow ma,
Kynth aswonn an lagha aga ewnderyow,
Yma aghorieth hwath,
Ha niggers yns i hwath.

156

The Slave Ship

A slave ship sets sail from the dark continent
With its human cargo to be sold
Like meat in the new world.
Locked in the hold,
Chained together in the dark
And suffocating in the fetid air,
Frightened and angry.
Women and children raped by the crew,
The dead thrown overboard to lighten the load.
After all, they're only niggers.
Not even human really.

These days,
Though the law may recognise their rights,
The bigotry remains,
And they're just niggers.

An Divres

Wosa tri henedh yn-mes a'n vammvro
Ha herdh-vegys gans gowyow ha plontyans,
Kellys yn tien yw an hevelepter.
Megys aval onan a'n estrenyon
Mes nevra yn tre yn hwir,
Owth assaya heb sewena dhe omfyttya,
Estren yn bro astranj.
Ow kwandra heb mynnas y'n tewlder heb worfenn,
Kellys ha kemmyskys,
Owth omdhiskwedhes heb lergh
Yn kethyans anvlasus an Sowson,
Dempnys dhe vywnans a ahwer
Toll du anken
Heb golow a waytyans.

Mes, an flamm a vyw hwath,
A'y worwedh yn kosk, down y'n enev
Bys pan dhasenowi
Ow tasserghi avel finiks
Diworth an lusow a dhesper
Dhe splanna aval golowva
Ow kevarwoedha an fordh
War vyaj a dhastikudhans,
Pergherinses dhe'n henvro,
Ha'n kynsa kammow prederus yn Kernow
A dhre amovyans desempis,
Daskesunyans lowenek,
Aval flogh kellys, kevys arta
Ha synsys yn diwvregh garadow y vamm,
Amovyans a longya,
Wortiwedh,
Y teuvev tre.

The Exile

After three generations away from the homeland
And force fed on a diet of lies and propaganda,
All sense of identity is lost.
Raised as one of the strangers,
But never truly at home,
Trying, yet unable to fit in,
A stranger in a strange land.
Drifting in eternal darkness,
Lost and confused,
Disappearing without trace
In the bland sameness of the Saxons,
Condemned to a life sentence of sorrow,
A black hole of misery
With no light of hope.

Yet, the flame remains alive,
Lying dormant deep within the soul
Until it reignites
Rising like a phoenix
From the ashes of despair
To shine like a beacon
Guiding the way
On a journey of rediscovery.
A pilgrimage to the old country
And the first tentative steps in Kernow
Bring a sudden rush of emotion,
A joyous reunion,
Like a lost child, found
Held in its mother's loving arms,
A sense of belonging,
At last,
I've come home.

Na Wra Omblegya

Gans Sen Pyran y'th kolonn kows Kernewek,
Gans Sen Pyran y'th kolonn pup-prys,
Gans Sen Pyran y'th kolonn kows Kernewek,
Kows Kernewek yn anedregus,
Na wra omblegya,
Na wra omblegya,
Na wra omblegya dhe'n yeth estren.

No Surrender

With St Piran in your heart speak in Cornish,
With St Piran in your heart always,
With St Piran in your heart speak in Cornish,
Speak in Cornish unrepentantly,
No surrender,
No surrender,
No surrender to the foreign tongue.

Chris Cadwur James

Tryflegow

I
Y hwelav dre dhewlagas loes
Orth gwel an koes
Termynn hir aban ty a leveris
Nyns yw oll kellys.
Hag an son gwyns a glappyas fest krev –
Ple'ma dha lev?

II
Unnweydh moy my a wovynnas
Ha ty a grias
My a'th kas ha my a'th kar
Ty a'n goer yn ta.
Pupprys yth esov omma –
Prag a wruss'ta mos alemma?

III
Ha ty a vynn dos ha bos koweth
Res yw dhymm leverel 'soweth!';
Ny allav vy gortos yn pellder
Awos ty vos ow melder.
Ha ty a drel dha fas
My a verk marnas kas.

Pan vydh an dydhyow ma gorfennys?
Ty a worthybis.
Na wrussons i dalleth
Nyns eson an keth.
Kellys ov lemmyn yn dagrow
Ha prederow hwerow.

Triads

I

I look through grey eyes
At the wood
It's a long time since you said
That all was not lost.
And the wind mutters very loudly –
Where is your voice?

II

Once more I ask
And you scream:
I hate you and I love you,
You know it well.
I'm always here –
Why did you go away?

III

So you want to become a friend
And I am bound to say 'tough!';
I will not wait in the wings
Because you are my love.
When you turn your face
I see only hate.

When will this finish?
You answer.
It did not begin,
We are not the same.
I am lost in tears
And bitter thoughts.

An Baner Anken

A wruss'ta gweles men logan
Gwithyas enev, se a-vann
Ow sevel war an woen yn-dann
An baner goesek anken?

A yll'ta blasa meth serrys
A'y sav war-vann a-ugh an bys
Y'n park ma ankow ha paynys
Rag baner goesek anken?

A wruss'ta klewes fleghes wann?
Nyns eus ragdha 'nas dughan
Nyns eus tre ragdha yn-dann
An baner goesek anken.

A yll'ta klewes anall yeyn
A gravas hag ow skwardya keyn?
Nyns eus powes vyth rag den
Yn-dann an baner anken.

Ha ty a sav war dir fest sans
An gwynsow gwyls orth an nans
A gudh an tros ifarn war-nans
An baner goesek anken.

Nyns esa kepar henna kyn
Teuth an kelyn gast Sowson
Ha lemmyn y res an avon hen
Yn-dann an baner anken.

Blas an goes, klyw an tros!
Blas an goes hag an anken!

The Flag of Grief

Did you ever see a logan stone,
The spirit's guard, a throne above
Standing on the moor below
The bloody flag of grief?

Can you smell the angry breath
Rising up high over the world
In this plain of pain and misery
For the bloody flag of grief?

Did you hear the powerless children?
There is nothing for them but sorrow,
There is no refuge for them under
The bloody flag of grief.

Can you feel the cold breath
Clawing and ripping your back?
All are defenceless
Below the flag of grief.

So you stand on very holy land,
The winds of a storm powering though the valley
To cover the sounds of hell under
The bloody flag of grief.

It wasn't like this before,
Then came those whelps of a Saxon whore
And now the old river flows
At the foot of the flag of grief.

Smell the blood, hear the noise!
Smell the blood and the misery.

Mernans

An ilow a dermynn a goedh kepar ha dagrow skoelys war leur prenn
lomm. Ha ty, gans an resyasow ow merwel a sterenn fethys a dreyl rag
an dewetha prys kyns plegya dhe'th planteys yeyn. Dha doemmyjyon
prederus gyllys y'n mannder a ankovva res heb govynn ha kemmerys
heb gras. Wor'tiwedh, an kan bywnans ha mernans a droyll y'th
kyrghynn ha'th megi yn unn keles dha vernans dha honan yn
kessenyans toellek ev a gram warnas kepar ha amm anvyw. Mes, ha
merwydh y'n tewlder splann a gosoleth, na wre'ta mos ahanan gans spit
dhe dyller kernwhili awos ni dhe vos gyllys yn dha gommolenn vras
ynwedh.

Death

The music of time falls like wasted tears onto a bare wooden floor. And you, with the dying rhythms of a vanished star turn for the last time before bowing to your cold planets. Your careful warmth lost in the void of forgetfulness freely given and cheaply taken. Finally, the song of life and death spins around you and smothers you hiding your own death in a deceitful harmony it crawls on you like a lifeless kiss. But, as you die in the shining darkness of tranquility, you do not go spitefully from us to a lonely place, because we are also lost in your vast cloud.

Gari Retallack

Yeth Ow Thas

War an fordh dhe Gernow
Gans gerlyver kres,
Lyver poes, lyver tew,
Skoes kolonnek yw

War an fordh dh'ow thre
Gans awen awenek,
Kledha lymm, kledha gwir,
Fayntys gwell bydh war.

Tremmenyas gwann ov, my a woer,
Moryonen war Bow Sows an borr.
Mes gans ow skoes ha gans ow hledha,
Nyns eus own dhymm.

My Father's Language

On the way to Cornwall,
with an intermediate dictionary,
a heavy book, a thick book,
it is a brave shield.

On my way to my home
with an uplifting inspiration,
a sharp sword, a true sword,
deceits had better take care.

I am a weak traveller, I know,
an ant on the fat of England.
But with my shield and with my sword,
I have no fear.

Alan M. Kent

Chapel Tolooarn, Metten Nadeleck

An re leal, madn an re wag, re theath
the woslowas worth drelgye'n pregowther
er hag evan a e dor gwlaneck down.

Dren tewlegean mons o toas, dan fenestrow
flehes es o pales en whels rag royow.
Denargh en lagas squeth, pendropya wolcum.

Hag ot an re leal en neves:
Scottie an Post, cane vethys en a lev creg.
An Doctour W. re anallas er then organ.

An Vestres Y, mam en Israel, pedn en gwisc pot te,
An Mester han Vestres D. thort cour an lythergee,
myrgh hap gour mes gans flo en tevry.

An Mester W. leun carengea ha dagrow, hep gwreag.
An Kyguer Lobb, ledn lour leave e gane
reg treghy an keeg en e wergy.

Arthur Bullock a henath treavedaze,
heerra pep noatedn es ouryow an mo.
Ha me, an mab scolliack, begh bez war ow holodn.

Ot an begel o kelwel e barra tha gana
en mease, hag ot en guream war un labm,
nen gana ha wherthyn, en ancambrengy po joy.

ha teeze ort gan lagatsha, lies gan kerun spern
nen vagla tho drea, tho dergosca, tho dhensol yar Guinea.
'Dordalla theugh,' ewe cry Ashley Norrish an Cyder.

Foxhole Chapel, Christmas Morning

The faithful ones, not the empty ones have come,
to listen to the monotonous drone of the preacher
fresh and broad in his deep woolly belly.

Through the darkness they come, under the windows
of children digging wildly for gifts.
Greeting in tired eyes, nodding welcomes.

And here are the faithful ones in the sanctuary:
Scottie the post master, song drowned in his hoarse voice.
Dr W giving fresh breathing to the organ.

Mrs Y, a mother in Israel, head in a tea-cosy,
Mr and and Mrs Respectable from the area of the post office,
daughter without husband, but properly up the spout.

Mr W, full of love and tears, without a wife.
Butcher Lobb – the voice of his song strong enough
to cut meat in his shop.

Arfur Bullock, the progeny of a founding father,
every note longer than the hours of the pre-dawn.
And I, the prodigal son, the world's burden on my heart.

And here's the shepherd calling his flock to sing
outside, and that is what we do at once,
singing and laughing, from embarrassment or joy.

And people stare at us, many with a hangover,
stumbling homeward, to nap, to chew turkey.
'Mornin' all,' cries Ashley Norrish the cider-head.

Polge po daou, ot gelles an re leall rho dreg
vease an yender del goath, thegory
tresorow M&S, the worthya 007.

A moment or two, and the faithful ones have gone home,
out of the cold, and as is fitting, to open
the treasures of M&S, then later, worship 007.

Aber Lydn

Clattra lovanow gooliou en par an Lydn,
ker klegh tewl dren nose,
whethel an lanwes.

Kens, rebban kenderow, goos teygeran o kelly
bes en strethou, sedar agon commiscas,
ynter govera ha devera.
Te wellas tykky-Dew hedar; yn sones
meras worto en powes,
plynchya dowaskell reethveladn vel blew-lagas gwels.
Dreas Mor Hawran ot doghajeth en Kembra,
teleryou mayth ejem o quary,
heb goothovose veean ne meyn en goles an geth avon.

An duder na gam mail en gwely
Gon dow o plenchya'n ledan vel an tykky-Dew
ha tynkyal vel clegh-paderow.
Ena'n precyous ne roll trobam mor
bes en dreheth an hinroze.

Lynmouth

Rattling of ropes of sails in the harbour of the Lyn,
choir of dark bells through the night,
story in the tide.

Earlier, by Watersmeet, orchids' blood spilling
into the streams, cedars mixed us
between rivuleting and trickling.
You saw a fragile butterfly; mesmerized
watching it at rest,
blinking orange wings like eyelashes of grass.
Beyond the Sea of Severn there is late afternoon in Wales,
places where we played
without knowing we should be stones in the same river bed.

That blackness enwraps us in bed,
both of us blinking wide like the butterfly
and tinkling like prayer bells.
Then delicately we roll towards the sea
into the reach of the dream.

Tikky-Dew en Boswynger

Poylann war bedn pin,
enevow diberthes war enes en More Creas,
trelyance dien, lub gwedh tho wer,
tedn an crown,
corfow pares tho dartha,
distrewy coogadnow clorform,
formya lagaseskelly
yn polgedn skyttra crehyn lagas.

Ot ragdroan ne omfeervya tho lappya
blegyon sugra go roath, trelya
tho roazer gleeth,
dastowedner golow,
meledna ez skerow amanen.

Butterfly at Boswinger

Pollen on the head of a pin,
separated souls on an island, in the Sea of Peace,
complete transformation, slush white into green,
taut the skin,
bodies ready to burst,
destroying chloroform shells,
creating eye-wings
in the tiny instant of the fluttering of eyelids.

Here is a proboscis forming itself to lick
flowers of sugar form, becoming
a nectar of dew,
a reflection of light,
yellow like slivers of butter.

Hanow Difednes

Nag es co thes an gwas thort Nanpean?
Ea. Gwas tane en coludn, menwarth war vean?

Nag es co thes an keath gwas en wheal?
Ea. Gwas an cres rugby, en praze hag en gweal?

Nag es co thes peth lavaras ben an gwas?
Ea. Boaz whans he gwelles en beth glase?

Nag es co thes cobal touvyes yn pyt Carpalla?
Ea. Eve scattyas gwas Trudge war am challa?

Nag es co thes de gollas a meel theathn an scoal?
Ea. Hag eve ena whathe o quare foal?

Nag es co thes na oothye va peoo o e dase?
Ea. Hep gallus gothevel gweer mase?

Nag es co thes dell gawas e pryson en oaze?
Ea. Ugge latha e reagne hae flow an gloase?

Nag es co thes del worras e lovan dro the lonk?
Nag es. Sure – fatal adgeoan ni loral mar stronk?

Taboo Subject

Dun't you remember the boy from Nanpean?
'Es. Wudn' a the boy with fire in his heart, a smile on his gob?

Dun't you remember the same at work?
'Es. Wudn' a the one with the rugby shirt everywhere he went?

Dun't you remember what the boy's maid said?
'Es. That he wanted to see her in a fresh grave?

Dun't you remember that 'ee 'eaved a knife in Carpalla pit?
'Es. Wudn' a the one who gave boy Trudge a hit?

Dun't you remember he lost a thousand days from school?
'Es. And even when he was there, playing the fool?

Dun't you remember he didn't knaw who was his father?
'Es. And that he cudn' bear the truth?

Dun't you remember he got given Life?
'Es. Wun't it after killing his wife and chield in agony?

Dun't you remember how he put a rope 'round his throat?
No, for sure. How would I ever knaw such a scoundrel?

Leav an Nyer Le

Te lavar nag on ne pobel.
Me lavar dees tho sevel gon ne.

Te lavar nag es taves gon ne.
Me lavar dees tho glappia gon ne.

Te lavar nag es ore gon ne.
Me lavar dees tho holyan avon genna ve.

Te lavar nag es ystory gon ne.
Me lavar dees tho veraz en tro genna ve.

Te lavar nag es syvylta gon ne.
Me lavar dees tho wosloowas urtan ne.

Te lavar nag es lahys gon ne.
Me lavar dees thon Senath.

Te lavar nag on ne tra veeth.
Me lavar vel on ne pep tra oll.

Te lavar gelles yu.
Me lavar keves yu.

Te lavar devys ough whe.
Me lavar gweervose on ne.

Te lavar nen deur nag onan.
Me lavar ma tan edn yolodn.

Me lavar te fell gon lesta.
Gwell thes goothvose hedna lebmen.

Minority Retort

You d'say we're not a people.
I d'say come and join us.

You d'say we've no language.
I d'say come and speak with us.

You d'say we've no border.
I d'say come and walk the river with me.

You d'say we've no history.
I d'say come and look back with me.

You d'say we've no culture.
I d'say come and listen to us.

You d'say we've no laws.
I d'say come to Convocation.

You d'say we're nothing.
I d'say we're everything.

You d'say it's gone.
I d'say I have found it.

You d'say we're invention.
I d'say we're real.

You d'say no one cares.
I d'say it form the heart.

I d'say you won't stop us.
Betterfit you d'knaw 'un now.

Kernopalooza Rap

Kernow ew younk ha Kernow ew noweth.
Ma Kernow lebmal rag bownans coweth.
Ma'n tellar whirni, thew kistan arrans.
Troil brauz prest kerna ragon kerens.

Nakevo an seinz ha'n vuyglenarian
Na judgio an duchy coynt, why murian.
Moth esta moez Camburn younk,
Dhom lagas ve che, vedh per vlounk.

Kernow ew younk ha Kernow ew noweth.
Ma Kernow lebmal rag bownans coweth.

Ma surfers ha muzzi war an treath.
Ma'n moar en ogas keniffer dedh.
Comero goz bord, fystenno dha'n howl.
En Towanblistri, thew hedna an tole.

Kernow ew younk ha Kernow ew noweth.
Ma Kernow lebmal rag bownans coweth.

Ea, ma tavas dha why, dha goz hunnen.
Ha wos oll an whiddlow ma bes onen.
Nag ew tavas rag tiz coth an en ednak.
Comero tabm, ma sawarn enwedgak.

Kernow ew younk ha Kernow ew noweth.
Ma Kernow lebmal rag bownans coweth.

Ha'n muzack obma, tua Pedn an Wlas.
Ew peath covathak, a ledia an beaz.
Gabba, grunge, rave, rock, drum ha forbordan.
Ea, ma Kernow seni carra cordan.

Kernow ew younk ha Kernow ew noweth.
Ma Kernow lebmal rag bownans coweth.

Kernopalooza Rap

See, Cornwall is young, and Cornwall is new.
Cornwall is kickin' for me and for you.
The place is buzzin', it's a treasure box.
A serious party, it always rocks.

Forget all your Smugglers and every Saint.
Don't you be judging this Duchy as quaint.
If y'straight outta' Camborne, then you're cool,
because if you know Cornwall, then you rule.

See, Cornwall is young, and Cornwall is new.
Cornwall is kickin' for me and for you.

Then there are surfers, babes, down on the beach.
In Cornwall, sea, sun and surf are easy to reach.
So go grab a board and run to the sun.
I'm tellin' ya – Newquay's cool for everyone.

See, Cornwall is young, and Cornwall is new.
Cornwall is kickin' for me and for you.

You've got a language there all of your own.
A happenin' lingo in this Kernow zone.
It's not just for old people, it's there for you,
so get out there sister and learn some too.

See, Cornwall is young, and Cornwall is new.
Cornwall is kickin' for me and for you.

There's the best music at this Land's End.
Sounds hardcore enough to set a new trend.
There's gabba, grunge, rave, rock, kickin' drum and bass.
See, in this Celtic place, we set the pace.

See, Cornwall is young, and Cornwall is new.
Cornwall is kickin' for me and for you.

Ma downssow mein soaz, teller brav,
fentidniow hudol ha nozow hav.
Ma clowans mystical dhur an tir
ke valsa mescack, che ore drew gwir.

Kernow ew younk ha Kernow ew noweth.
Ma Kernow lebmal rag bownans coweth.
Man tellar whirni, thew kistan arrans.
Troil brauz prest kerna ragon kerens.

Della, lavarro dhem arta, drew an questyon' na?
"Fatel ew Kernow en deethiow ma?"

Ha why as senges bes Arthur ha hogednow...

184

You've got major cool places like ancients sites,
groovy magical wells and hot summer nights.
And there's a mystic vibe goin' on too.
So don't dis it boy – you know it's true.

See, Cornwall is young, and Cornwall is new.
Cornwall is kickin' for me and for you.
The place is buzzin', it's a treasure box.
A serious party, it always rocks.

So tell me, what was that question again?
"What's Cornwall like these days?"

And you thought it was nothing more than King Arthur
and pasties...

Katrina Waters

An Sin

An venyn a viras orth an ebrenn ynk glas.
Hi a wortas y'n hen bras,
kynth o oer an gwynsow
hi a wiskas yn pows tanow.
Yth esa hi ow hwilas an sterenn
may fo an sin.

An mor a hanas yn tawesek yn-dann an als,
ow frosa yn hag yn-mes diworth an hen val.
Hy dowlagas a dhallethas degea
ha hy skwithter a wrug hy hudha.
Dell goskas hi, y hwrug resek an sterenn
a-dreus an ebrenn.

The Sign

The woman looked at the ink-blue sky.
She waited in the ancient meadow,
although the wind was bitterly cold
she was dressed in flimsy clothes.
She was searching for the star
which might be the sign.

The sea whispered quietly beneath the cliffs,
flowing in and out of the ancient mine.
Her eyes began to close
and tiredness enveloped her.
As she slept, the star raced
across the sky.

Kellys

My a wra kerdhes
yn lent, a dreus an treth,
yn ynn govhe...

Dha dhowlagas
mar dhown ha hudel avel an mor,
yma dha wols a nev
ow kanna aval an loer...

Ass my a wrug
dha gara!
Mes lemmyn, ty a wra gasa,
ytho, soweth, kellys os ta.

Lost

I walk
slowly across the beach,
remembering...

Your eyes
as deep and enchanting as the sea,
your heavenly hair,
shining like the moon...

How I
loved you!
But now, you are leaving,
so, alas, you are lost.

Matthew Clarke

Souder Yowynk

An gwin a lenter y'n gantolgann.
Souder yowynk a hunros y'n gaslann
A-dro dh'y gares usi pell dhe-ves.
Unn gas moy a dhre an jydh a nes.
Hunrosa a wra a dus a vri aga holonn dha,
Hunrosa yn klor a'y gares neb usi dres an mor.

Kavoes kar re wrug hi nes dh'y threv
Souder yowynk re gollas y gares ev
Ymava ow merwel war an vre yn hons
Y vernans ow skoellya an diwettha chons
Merwel a wra, hy hanow hwystrys der y anall wann
Merwel a wra, y gares lowen dhedhi skians mann.

Yma'n vowes ow tevi brassa hweg hy min.
Yma mamm-wynn ow kewsel a-dro dhe'n gwella gwin.
Hunros yma dhedhi hi a'n souder koll.
Diweres yw hi erbyn kov a oell.
Hunrosa a wra a dus a vri aga holonn dha,
Hunrosa yn klor hy har a goedhas pur bell dres an mor.

Young Soldier

The wine gleams in the bright candle-light.
A young soldier dreams in the battlefield
About his sweetheart who is far away.
One more battle will bring the day closer.
He dreams of people of renown and courage,
Dreams gently of his sweetheart who is over the sea.

She has found a lover closer to her home.
A young soldier has lost his sweetheart.
He is dying on the hill yonder.
His death wasting the last chance.
He dies, her name whispered in his weak breath.
He dies, his sweetheart happy without any knowledge.

The girl with the sweet face is growing up.
Her grandmother is speaking about the best wine.
She has a dream of the lost soldier.
She is helpless against the memory of weeping.
She dreams of people of renown and courage,
Dreams gently of her lover who fell far across the sea.

Talvann

Tir rag displegyans.
An arwoedh yw hen.
Fordh entra yw lettys
Gans gwiver ha men.
Dheragdha 'ma gwerthor
Ha bleujennow fest splann
Hag y hyllir y weles,
War an fordh dhe Dalvann.

An prys yw ankevyes
Pan wonethas an hwel
– Crofti Gogledh –
Gans stennoryon pur lel.
Lemmyn le da yw
Rag stroellya pub rann.
Hag y hyllir y weles
War an fordh dhe Dalvann.

An hyns dhiworth Poll
O kosel ha glas,
Mes lemmyn 'th yw skwardys
Gans fordh euthek bras.
Hebask nyns yw kevys,
Nag yn chi nag yn lann.
Hag y hyllir y glywes
War an fordh dhe Dalvann.

Tenkys a vona.
Park negys y fydh,
Arwoedh dynnerghi,
'Dro dhodho skeuswydh.
Tru nyns eus soedhva,
Travydh dh'y wul mann.
Hag y hyllir y gelli
War an fordh dhe Dalvann.

Tolvaddon

Land for development.
The sign is old.
The entrance road is blocked
With wire and stone.
In front of them is a salesman
And very fine flowers,
And it can be seen
On the way to Tolvaddon.

The time is forgotten
When the mine was worked
– North Crofty –
By very trusty tinners.
Now it is a good place
To fill up with litter.
And it can be seen
On the way to Tolvaddon.

The way from Pool
Was quiet and green,
But now it is torn
By a fearfully great road.
No calm is to be found,
Whether in house or in churchyard.
And it can be heard
On the way to Tolvaddon.

A destiny of cash.
There will be a business park,
A welcome sign,
With sheltering trees around it.
Alas, there is no office,
Nothing to do at all.
And it can be missed
On the way to Tolvaddon.

Benjamin Bruch

an kynsa

ny allav leverel
py dydh y tallathas
ow hwans mar anfeusik
anodho

mes megys gans hwansow
ow hwilas kerensa
ow horf gans y gorf,
my a'n karas

ow kweles y gorf
yn y sevel,
y waya,
y resek –
pub esel o perfeyth

y dhiwarr geherek ha blewek, ystynnys,
mar grev ha mar nerthek dheragdho,

ha'y dhiwleuv mar gonnyk ha freth y'ga gwaya,
ha'y dhiwvregh a ambosa skovva,

ha gwel y dhewlagas mar las pan y's gwelyn,
dew nev
owth igeris dheragov

ha geryow a gevis,
ha geryow a skoellis
ow skrifa a dhownder ow hwansow

ha my yn y gyrghynn,
an geryow y'm ganow –
ha my heb an galloes
dhe gewsel

194

the first

I can't say
what day it began,
my desire, my ill-fated yearning
to have him

but fed by desires
and searching for love,
for my body with his,
I did love him

the sight of his body
when standing,
when moving,
when running –
each member perfection

his two legs so muscled and hairy, extended,
so strong and so potent before him,

his two hands so clever and deft in their motions,
his two arms that promised me shelter,

the sight of his two sky-blue eyes when I'd seen them,
twin heavens that
opened before me

and words I discovered,
and words, too, I poured forth,
to write of my deepest desires

and when in his presence,
the words in my mouth –
I lost then the power
to speak them

mes klywes a wrug ev
an pyth na leveris;
konvedhes a wrug
ow gologow

ha my pan y'n gwelyn
y helgha a wren vy
hag ev pan y'm gweli
y fia

ha dyfh wosa dydh

agan taw ni a devi
ha nevra ny glywen
y dava

ha kyn nag ens kewsys
an geryow yntredhon
a besyas
a'n rannas
bynari

but still he did hear it,
the thing left unspoken;
he understood well
my attentions

and when I would see him
I'd try to pursue him
and when he would see me,
he'd flee me

and day after day passed

our silence increasing,
and never would I feel him
touch me

and though left unspoken
the words still between us
endured
to divide us
forever

Talat Chaudri

Dhe Dhybarth an Fordhow?

My a wovyn py hyllyf-vy mos
lemmyn mara mynny deryvas
nep le; fatel ny wodhesta bos
dhym avel an golom yn lagas
an nef da, kynth os dygabester
nefra dhe vos hebof-vy arta
y'n jeth splan kepar del vynnysta
Trawythyow y coth predery peur
teuffo dhe-wyr dybarth an fordhow.

My a dyby ny ve yndelma;
bos genes a gemer ow thavas
adherak gwel ha dre wder a
hag ow trelya lywyow yn lagas
an howl glew. Dha fordhow a sommys
a'm gwra dha vyras aval pen-bron.
Ytho wreta mos mes a'w holon
Hag a grogen wak dhe scul tewlys?
Yw hy hep wow dybarth an fordhow?

To the Parting of the Ways?

I ask where I can go
if you will indicate
any place; how is it that you cannot be
like the dove in the eye for me
of the good heaven, although you are unfettered,
never to be without me again
in the bright day as you willed.
Sometimes, it is fitting to consider when
the parting of the ways will indeed come.

I supposed that it would not be like this;
my tongue takes being with you
before my sight and through glass
and changes colours in the eye
of the bright sun. Your shifting ways
make me look a fool.
Will you, then, go out of my heart
and throw me away like an empty shell?
Is it, in truth, the parting of the ways?

Biographies

Wella Brown b.1917
Author of stories, novels and books, including *A Grammar of Modern Cornish* (1984), his bardic name is Crenor ('Quaker').

Nerth Medhel/Soft Strength. Author's collection.

Richard Gendall b.1924
Founder of the Cornish magazine *An Lef* (later *An Lef Kernewek*) he is the author of numerous textbooks, grammars and dictionaries, and pioneer of the modern Cornish song. His most recent publications include *A New Dictionary of Modern Cornish* (1998) and *Tavas a Ragadazow/The Language of My Forefathers* (2000). His bardic name is Gelvynak ('Curlew').

An Yrth/The Snow. Author's collection.
Moaz Lowz/Adrift. Craig Weatherhill *(1995) Cornish Place Names and Language,* Wilmslow: Sigma, p.22.
Stearen Lesky/Shooting Star. Ibid., p.103.
Ula an Cooz/The Wood Owl. Ibid., p.151.

Richard Jenkin 1925–2002
Jenkin was a founder member of the Cornish nationalist party Mebyon Kernow and fought the European Election of 1979 as their first European candidate. He was co-editor of the magazine *New Cornwall* and editor of the Cornish language magazine *Delyow Derow/Oak Leaves*. His bardic name was Map Dyvroeth ('Son of Exile') and he was twice Grand Bard of the Cornish Gorseth.

Yma Cowas Ow-tegensewa/A Shower is Looming. (1992) *Delyow Derow/Oak Leaves*, No.9, pp.16–17.
Lef y'n Nos/Voice in the Night. Author's collection.

Jowann Richards 1926–2005

By profession a chemical engineer and technical author, Richards was one of the most prolific writers of novels, short stories and poems in Cornish. His bardic name is Mab Roswern ('Son of Rosewarne').

Kan an Vowes Yowynk/Song of the Young Girl. Author's collection.

Ann Trevenen Jenkin b.1930

A founder member of Mebyon Kernow, she has been active for many years within the pan-Celtic movement, travelling widely across the world promoting Cornwall. In 1997 she became the first woman Grand Bard of the Cornish Gorseth. Her bardic name is Bryallen ('Primrose').

Hal Dart/Dartmoor. Ann Trevenen Jenkin (2005) *Crygon Kernow Ogas ha Pell/Cornish Ripples Near and Far,* Leedstown: Noonvares Press, p.30. *Mernans/Death.* Ibid., pp.32–3.

Donald R. Rawe b.1930

Born in Padstow, Rawe founded the Cornish publishing house Lodenek Press in 1970. A historian and folklorist, he is also the author of a number of dramas, stories and poems on Cornish themes. His bardic name is Scryfor Lanwedoc ('Writer of Padstow').

An Skyla dhe Vos/The Reason for Being. Author's collection.
Pysadow rak Kernow yn Vledhen 2000 [esrann]/Prayer for Cornwall in the Year 2000 [extract]. Author's collection.
Geryow Kernewek/Cornish Words. Author's collection.

Michael Palmer 1936–2005

Michael Palmer was a clergyman, novelist and short-story writer. His bardic name was Pryeryn Tyr Sans ('Pilgrim of the Holy Land').

An Gour Gwedhow Yowynk/The Young Widower. Author's collection.

William Morris b.1937

Born in West Cornwall, he was one of the original members of the Cornish Language Board and editor of the volume *Gorsedd Poems* (1976). He lives in London and has written stories in English, Cornish, Welsh and German. His bardic name is Haldreyn ('Moor of Thorns')

Nos Gwavek/Winter Night. Author's collection.

Antony Snell b.1938
A science teacher, Tony Snell lives in Oxford. He has studied the craft of the early Celtic poets as a model for disciplined metrical and conceptual work. His bardic name is Gwas Kervardhu ('December's Man').

Travydh Trogh/Nothing Broken. Author's collection.
Resek Nos/Night Run. Author's collection.
Dy'Goel Felyon Oll 1995/All Fools' Day 1995. Author's collection.
'Medh Hykka/Said Dick. Author's collection.
Marghak an Mordardh/Knight of the Surf. Author's collection.
Klappkodh/Mobile Phone. Author's collection.

Jori Ansell b.1941
Ansell is a long-standing teacher of Cornish, and works professionally as a translator. He is a former Grand Bard of the Cornish Gorseth.

Trevas/Harvest. Author's collection.

Brian Webb 1941–1986
Singer and songwriter. *Ow Avon Splann* became one of the most popular songs in the Cornish language. His early death deprived Cornwall of a wealth of verse and song. His bardic name was Brythennek ('Freckled One').

Ow Avon Splann. (1996) *Kanow Kernewek,* Grampound Road: Cornish Language Fellowship.

N.J.A. Williams b.1942
A Celtic scholar who has taught at the University of Liverpool and University College, Dublin, he has published several works in the field of Irish Studies. He is the author of *Cornish Today: An Examination of the Revived Language* (1995) and *Clappya Kernowek: An Introduction to Unified Cornish Revived* (1997). He takes the bardic name Golvan ('Sparrow').

An Lowarth Cosel [esrann]/The Quiet Garden [extract]. Author's collection.

Ken George b.1947
George is a respected scholar of Cornish, active in the Cornish Language Board, and author of *The Pronunciation and Spelling of Revived Cornish* (1986), *The New Standard Cornish Dictionary* (1998) and the *English/Cornish Mini-Dictionary* (2005)

An Velin Goth/The Old Mill. Author's collection.
Mester an Porth/The Harbour Master. Author's collection.

Mick Paynter b.1948
Mick Paynter was born in St Ives and was educated at Humphry Davy School, Penzance, and at the University of Newcastle. He works in Penzance as a Revenue Officer. His bardic name is Skogynn Pryv ('Worm's Fool').

Divroans 1890/Diaspora 1890. Mick Paynter (2000) *A Crowd of Banners: Verses in Cornish,* St. Ives: Mick Paynter, pp.26–7.
Ple'ma'an Tus Bras Agan Domhwelans?/Where are the Big People of Our Revolution? Ibid., pp.36–7.
Rag Primo Levi/For Primo Levi. Mick Paynter (n.d.) *Gwersyow Arta/Verses Again.* St. Ives. Mick Paynter, pp.2–3.
Gorhel Terrys/A Broken Ship. Mick Paynter (2004) *And all the World Our Patch: Cornish Language Poems and others,* Redruth: Palores, pp.4–5.
Bresel Tas/Dad's War. Ibid., pp.18–19.
Ha Blair ha Bush/Blair and Bush. Ibid., pp.24–25.

Julyan Holmes b.1948
Holmes is a long-standing scholar of Cornish and a political activist. He is currently researching Edward Lhuyd's work on the Cornish language. Holmes' bardic name is Blew Melen ('Yellow Hair').

An Taves Hen/The Old Language. Author's collection.
Kosovo/Kosovo. Author's collection.

Pawl Dunbar b.1948
Pawl Dunbar lives in Liskeard and runs a bookshop dedicated to Cornish culture. In the past he has worked as a shipwright, and was editor of the political magazine *Kernow* between 1986 and 1996. His bardic name is Dinas ('Fortress').

Bora Mor/Early Morning at Sea. Author's collection.
Treth Banna/Banna Strand. Author's collection.

Ray Chubb b.1949
Chubb is a publisher, bookseller and director of Agan Tavas, the Society for the Promotion of the Cornish Language. His bardic name is Map Essa ('Son of Saltash').

An Als Abarth Cleth/The North Cliff. Author's collection.

Graham Sandercock b.1950
A teacher by profession, Sandercock has made an huge contribution to contemporary Cornish culture. He has edited *An Gannas* – the longest running Cornish-language magazine – since 1977 and written numerous publications, including *Holyewgh an Lergh/Cornish This Way* (1993) and *The First Thousand Words in Cornish* (1994). He is also a musician and singer; his bardic name is Gwas Connoc ('Fellow of Boconnock').

Chi an Hordh/The House of the Ram. Graham Sandercock (1990) *Geryow,* Cornwall: Kowethas an Yeth Kernewek, p.18.
Poll Pri/Clay Pit. Ibid., pp.62–3.
Kataloni/Catalonia. Ibid., p.76.

Philip Chadwick b.1950
A philologist and genealogist, Chadwick learnt Cornish at the City Literary Institute. He is currently President of the London Association for Celtic Education.

Dursonyowdhis/God Sound You. Author's collection.
Ervirans Hav/Summer's Resolution. Author's collection.

Tim Saunders b.1952
Saunders studied Celtic Studies at the University of Wales, Aberystwyth, and has published poetry, journalism and fiction in Welsh, Irish, Breton as well as in Cornish. His bardic name Bardh Gwerin ('People's Poet').

An Pennlanw/The High Tide. Tim Saunders (1999) *The High Tide: Collected Poems in Cornish 1974–1999,* London: Francis Boutle, pp.24–9.
Tavow/Touches. Ibid., pp.44–5.

Awedh [esrann]/Watercourse [extract]. Tim Saunders/Alan M. Kent
Awedh/Watercourse. London: Francis Boutle. To be published in 2007.
An Ros Du/Blackheath. Tim Saunders (2003) *Gol Snag Bud ha Gweryow
Whath*, Portreath: Spyrys a Gernow, pp.1–2.
Gol Snag Bud/Bude Jazz Festival. Ibid., pp.23–4.
An Edenva/The Eden Project. Ibid., pp.25–6.

Judith Larham b.1956
Larham is a lecturer in further and adult education. Her bardic name is
Moren Dur ('Maid of Steele').

Pysadow rag an Naw Kans/Prayer for the Nine Hundred. Author's
collection.

Neil Kennedy b.1959
Kennedy currently lives and works in Brittany. He was formerly a lecturer in Cultural Studies at University College, Falmouth. He is an
active teacher of Cornish and has produced several books and record-
ings for beginners. He published *Imagination in the Teaching of Cornish*
(2000) and has written several articles for Cornish Studies.

Try Flam a Dan/Three Flames of Fire. Author's collection.
An Vlewan Looz/The Grey Hair. Author's collection.
Meriasek/Meriasek. Auhor's collection.
Brilli a Clappia/Mackerel Talking. Featured as a drum and bass
arrangement in Helen Foster (dir.) (1998) *Kernopalooza!* Plymouth:
Carlton Westcountry Television.
An Brennik/The Limpets. Featured on Dalla (2001) *A Richer Vein*, St.
Agnes: Dalla.
Baner Vith/No Flag. Author's collection.

Cliff Stephens b.1961
Cliff Stephens works in the health service and lives near Truro. He
writes agitprop poetry in Cornish and is an active member of Kowethas
an Yeth Kernewek/The Cornish Language Board.

Kryjyans Nowydh/A New Religion. Cliff Stephens (1999) *Kernewek gans
Omdhalgh/Cornish with Attitude*. Cornwall: Kowethas an Yeth Kernewek,
pp.12–13.
Gorhel an Gethyon/The Slave Ship. Ibid., p.15.

An Divres/The Exile. Ibid., p.22–23.
Na Wra Omblegya/No Surrender. Ibid., p.27.

Chris Cadwur James b.1963

Cadwur James has worked as a musician, teacher and writer in London, the Middle East and Cornwall. He now lives near Redruth.

Tryflegow/Triads. Author's collection.
An Baner Anken/The Flag of Grief. Author's collection.
Mernans/Death. Author's collection.

Gari Retallack b.1964

A Lecturer in Adult Education, he has worked as a tutor in Philosophy, History and Literature for the Workers' Education Association. A former student of Cornish at the City Literary Institute, he has since become a tutor there.

Yeth Ow Thas/My Father's Language. Author's collection.

Alan M. Kent b.1967

Alan M. Kent was born in mid-Cornwall and was educated at the Universities of Cardiff and Exeter, gaining a doctorate in Cornish and Anglo-Cornish Literature. He now lectures in Literature for the Open University.

Chapel Tôlooarn, Metten Nadeleck/Foxhole Chapel, Christmas Morning.
Author's collection.
Aber Lydn/Lynmouth. Author's collection.
Tikky-Dew en Boswynger/Butterfly at Boswinger. Author's collection.
Hanow Difednes/Taboo Subject. Author's collection.
Leav an Nyer Le/Minority Retort. Author's collection.
Kernopalooza Rap. Helen Foster (dir.) (1998) *Kernopalooza!* Plymouth: Carlton Westcountry Television.

Katrina Waters b.1970

Born in Redruth, Waters is an analytical scientist. She is an active member of Mebyon Kernow, and has also had poetry published in English.

An Sin/The Sign. Author's collection.
Kellys/Lost. Author's collection.

Matthew Clarke b.1970
A journalist and newsreader, he has been an important figure in Cornish media, initiating news bulletins in Cornish on Pirate FM radio. He is also a musician, writing and playing songs in Cornish.

Souder Yowynk/Young Soldier. Author's collection.
Talvann/Tolvaddon. Author's collection.

Benjamin Bruch b.1973
Born in Wisconsin, USA, Bruch began studying Cornish in 1995 and was made a bard of the Cornish Gorseth by examination in the Cornish language three years later. He has written a number of short stories in Cornish. He recently completed a PhD in Celtic languages at Harvard.

an kynsa/the first. Author's collection.

Talat Chaudri b.1977
Chaudri is a researcher in Celtic Studies with interests in both archaeology and the theatre, who is currently researching the languages and literatures of the sixteenth century. He lives in Carmarthen.

Dhe Dhybarth an Fordhow?/To the Parting of the Ways? Author's collection.

Further Reading

Ably, Mark (2003) *Spoken Here: Travels Among Threatened Languages*, London: Heinemann.

Deacon, Bernard, Cole, Dick and Tregidga, Garry (2003) *Mebyon Kernow and Cornish Nationalism*, Cardiff: Welsh Academic Press.

Ellis, Peter Berresford (1974) *The Cornish Language and its Literature*, London and Boston: Routledge and Kegan Paul.

Gendall, Richard (2000) *Tavas a Ragadazow/The Language of My Forefathers*, Menheniot: Teer ha Tavas.

George, Ken (1986) *The Pronunciation and Spelling of Revived Cornish*, Cornwall: The Cornish Language Board.

– (2000) *Gerlyver Kernewek Kemmyn – An Gerlyver Kres: Kernewek-Sowsnek, Sowsnek-Kernewek/Cornish-English, English-Cornish Dictionary*, Cornwall: Kesva an Taves

Harvey, David C., Jones, Rhys, McInroy, Neil and Milligan, Christine (eds.) (2002) *Celtic Geographies: Old Culture, New Times*, London and New York: Routledge.

Hodge, Pol (1997) *Mouth on 'en like Dolcoath Shaft*, Lodenek Press: Padstow

Kent, Alan M. (1995) *Out of the Ordinalia*, St Austell: Lyonesse

– (2000) *The Literature of Cornwall: Continuity, Identity, Difference 1000–2000*, Bristol: Redcliffe.

– (ed.) (2000) *Voices from West Barbary: An Anthology of Anglo-Cornish Poetry 1549–1928*, London: Francis Boutle.

– (ed.) (2004) *The Dreamt Sea: An Anthology of Anglo-Cornish Poetry 1928–2004*, London: Francis Boutle.

– (2005) *Ordinalia, The Cornish Mystery Play Cycle: A Verse Translation*, London: Francis Boutle.

– and Saunders, Tim (eds.) (2000) *Looking at the Mermaid: A Reader in Cornish Literature 900–1900*, London: Francis Boutle.

Koch, John T. (ed.) (2005) *Celtic Culture: A Historical Encyclopedia*, Santa Barbara and Oxford: ABC-Clio

Moore, David W. (2005) *The Other British Isles*, Jefferson, North Carolina and London: McFarland.

Murdoch, Brian (1993) *Cornish Literature*, Cambridge: Brewer.

Nic Craith, Máiréad (ed.) (1996) *Watching One's Tongue: Aspects of Romance and Celtic Languages*, Liverpool: Liverpool University Press.

Payton, Philip (1992) *The Making of Modern Cornwall: Historical Experience and the Persistence of "Difference"*, Redruth: Dyllansow Truran.

Russell, Paul (1995) *An Introduction to the Celtic Languages*, Harlow: Longman

Saunders, Tim (1977) *Teithiau*, Talybont: Y Lolfra.

– (ed.) (1978) *Cornish is Fun! A new course in living Cornish by Richard Gendall*, Talybont: Y Lolfra.

– (ed.) (1999) *The Wheel: An Anthology of Modern Poetry in Cornish 1850–1980*, London: Francis Boutle.

Stalmaszczyk, Piotr (2005) *Celtic Presence: Studies in Celtic Languages and Literatures – Irish, Scottish Gaelic and Cornish*, Lodz : Lodz University Press

Tanner, Marcus (2004) *The Last of the Celts*, New Haven and London: Yale University Press.

Weatherhill, Craig (1995) *Cornish Place Names and Language*, Wilmslow: Sigma.

Weight, Richard (2002) *Patriots: National Identity in Britain 1940–2000*, London: Macmillan.

Williams, Derek (ed.) (2004) *Henry and Katharine Jenner: A Celebration of Cornwall's Culture, Language and Identity*, London: Francis Boutle.

Williams, N.J.A. (1995) *Cornish Today: An Examination of the Revived Language*, Sutton Coldfield: Kernewek dre Lyther.